Holy Hurt

UNDERSTANDING SPIRITUAL TRAUMA
and the PROCESS *of* HEALING

HILLARY L. McBRIDE, PhD

BrazosPress

a division of Baker Publishing Group
Grand Rapids, Michigan

Published by Brazos Press
a division of Baker Publishing Group
Grand Rapids, Michigan
BrazosPress.com

Printed in the United States of America

Library of Congress Cataloging-in-Publication Data
Names: McBride, Hillary L., author.
Title: Holy hurt : understanding spiritual trauma and the process of healing / Hillary L. McBride, PhD.
Description: Grand Rapids, Michigan : Brazos Press, a division of Baker Publishing Group, [2025] | Includes bibliographical references.
Identifiers: LCCN 2024036319 | ISBN 9781587436598 (paperback) | ISBN 9781587436604 (casebound) | ISBN 9781493449583 (ebook)
Subjects: LCSH: Psychic trauma—Religious aspects—Christianity. | Psychology, Religious.
Classification: LCC BV4461 .M33 2025 | DDC 259/.42—dc23/eng/20240905
LC record available at https://lccn.loc.gov/2024036319

Collage and cover design by Courtney Search

Some names or details of the people and situations described in this book have been changed or presented in composite form in order to ensure the privacy of those with whom the author has worked.

The author is represented by the Christopher Ferebee Agency, www.christopherferebee.com.

Baker Publishing Group publications use paper produced from sustainable forestry practices and postconsumer waste whenever possible.

25 26 27 28 29 30 31   7 6 5 4 3 2 1

To all our younger selves,
who needed to know then but can finally learn now:
you can listen to your body,
you can trust yourself,
and you are good at your core.

CONTENTS

INTRODUCTION

A few years ago, I found myself walking through a hardware store looking for a gardening tool. I had snaked my way through at least forty-two aisles, dragging my fingers along the metal baskets protruding on both sides of me just to hear the musical tones this created. It was taking forever. But that was the point. I was on an escape mission—otherwise known as an extended break—from writing the script for the *Holy/ Hurt* podcast, which was seven months overdue.

On this Friday morning, I had set aside time to finally dig into the project in a way I hadn't yet been able to commit myself to. But instead, I found myself magically transported to the hardware store looking for a very specific kind of spade. I wasn't avoiding only the writing. I was avoiding the email from my producer that had been sitting in my inbox for weeks, politely checking in to see how the project was going. I was avoiding talking about any of this with my therapist. This was my way of putting off remembering the stories connected to my own spiritual injuries, and the questions those memories brought to the surface.

There I was in aisle forty-two when "Undone (The Sweater Song)," the punk rock anthem by Weezer, came on. All I could do was throw my head back and laugh. "If you want to destroy my sweater, hold this thread as I walk away . . . I've come undone."[1] Tears rolled out of my eyes into my ears as I sang along, far louder than was normal in a public place. I couldn't escape the irony; unraveling was exactly what was happening inside me. These were my words, or the words I had been avoiding saying until that moment. A man walked into the aisle and turned on his heel as soon as he saw me. I'm sure I looked slightly unhinged.

I was there searching for a garden tool because I was afraid to pull on anything connected to my own experiences of spiritual trauma. I knew I couldn't write about spiritual trauma in any depth—couldn't read the research, tell the stories, or talk about the healing—without touching the places inside me connected to it all. I was afraid to pull the thread because what if, at the end of it, there was nothing left? What would it cost me? What would I lose of what had been familiar, of what had kept me safe?

I laugh-cried all the way home. I had processed various other traumas before, but this one had always been easier to talk about at a distance, when it was an idea, another person's story, a patient's healing journey that I could witness from the other side of the couch. But this seemed to strike deeper at my core, almost as if pulling on the thread of the memories would unravel my essence. I had no idea how much avoidance there was inside me related to these wounds, how much dissociation was masking my fear, until I saw month after month flipping by on the calendar and the project I had originally been excited to work on seemed uncharacteristically impossible to begin.

I asked my therapist during our session that week if we could go somewhere new, somewhere I was so reluctant to go that I'd convinced myself I didn't need to go there at all. That was also the week I could finally sit down at the computer and begin to write. When my avoidance began to thaw, underneath it I found painfulness. Getting close to tender places allowed me to get close to my heart, and what I found was not only pain but also courage and creativity. Numbing one meant numbing both.

◆ ◆ ◆

In working on this project, first in the form of collecting ideas for the *Holy/Hurt* podcast and then in writing this book, I found more threads to pull than I knew were there. I have lost count of how many times I felt the squeeze in my chest while I was working, or the bottom of my stomach seemingly drop out of my body. How many times I felt the urge to set the entire project aside, and with it all the painful places it connected me to inside of myself. But being connected to myself, pain and all, was the only way I wanted to write this, knowing that this material might cause similar discomfort for you too, knowing that you might also be picking this up because you found yourself in some metaphorical hardware store doing anything you could not to pull on those threads. As I confronted my self-protective measures—all my avoidance and dissociation around these pockets of pain—I understood again how the strength of our defenses against discomfort is equal in measure to the intensity of the discomfort we are defending against.

The more I came to understand how painful spiritual trauma is, the more I wanted you, reader, to feel accompanied in exploring it. I wanted you to know that the places you are about to go I have been willing to go as well. I hope that in the moments when reading this book feels challenging you can imagine me there with you, walking this path alongside you, and that this helps to dispel the feelings of aloneness that rise up for you. Whether through writing, reading, or speaking to these injuries living inside us, to turn toward them at all is to see a glimmer of the courageous self who lives inside, who knows there is more for us on the other side of looking at what was previously unbearable to acknowledge.

To give you a better sense of what is coming, I want you to know a few things before we go any further. First, this book was created for those with lived experience of spiritual trauma. What has been used to hurt you in the past can come with significant and sometimes surprising physiological reactions when you encounter the same words, behaviors, or processes in the present. With this in mind, I made the decision *not to use prayer, references to Scripture, or explicitly Christian language.* I don't know what specifically was used to harm you or how the legacy of that harm still lives in you, so I cannot guarantee that reading this will feel easy. But I do want you to know that there will not be any altar calls or surprising prayers and that I trust you to know when you have had enough or need to take a break. If you are not sure about that, your body will tell you. If the only thing you take away from reading this book is that you got to do so in a way that allowed you to trust yourself more, I will be so grateful.

Second, if you are actively part of a faith community or find yourself within the Christian tradition and are reading this to better understand what spiritual trauma is and how it impacts those around you, I am so glad you are here. You might notice that although this book is about spiritual trauma, spiritual practices and theological or religious ways of making sense of pain and trauma are decidedly absent. I hope based on the previous comment that this makes sense. Although some of the material may be uncomfortable or new to you, I invite you to stay through the discomfort, take breaks as you need, and hold a posture of openness and curiosity. I believe that your ability to learn about spiritual trauma will help you create healthier communities and love your neighbor with more compassion and wisdom. It is so important you are here.

◆ ◆ ◆

This book emerged out of an audio project I did with Sanctuary Mental Health in late 2023. An important part of that project was the audio-recorded conversations I had with colleagues, experts, and friends about spiritual trauma, which were included in each episode. Through these conversations, which represent different experiences and perspectives, not only did my understanding about spiritual trauma become richer, but I found myself less alone. I imagine you might feel the same way, so I have included portions of these interviews at the end of each chapter. Because the text was taken from recorded audio conversations, minor changes have been made to the original interviews in the interest of readability. Each of these people has so much more to say than is captured here, so please seek out the other places where their voices can be heard.

ONE

The House Is Haunted

Shortly after my parents were married, they moved to the West Coast. Both of them left behind big families who farmed in the prairies. When they started life over out West, they joined a warm church community off a central Vancouver thoroughfare. There were choirs with royal blue robes, youth groups, barbecues in parks, all-hands-on-deck musicals at Christmas, and a community that continued to grow as the families that belonged to it did too. A new building was built with the pulpit at the very center of the building, a signal of what mattered most to that church: the Word of God.

When I reflect back on my childhood years, this church is a central feature. I never knew a time without it. Because of the distance between my parents and their families in another province, this community was in a sense the most tangible expression of family we had. At birthdays and Christmas, their cards and gifts filled our home. Their poppyseed cake for dessert midweek anchored us in place until we saw each other again. I'd have one auntie's hand smacking my hand away just as I found the stash of cookies in the church kitchen while another auntie was sneaking the very same cookies to me through her billowing skirt pockets when no one was looking. This was my family.

Then, half of them were gone. It seemed as though this happened overnight, but I can't remember if that was the reality or just what it felt like. My confusion reflected the chaos around me, and I felt the loss of a rich relational world that seemingly collapsed overnight. I never saw some of those people again.

If you were watching a movie of my memories of that place and those people, this is where the film would take on a distinctly dull tone—as if everything was covered by a thin layer of dust—the laughter sparse and muffled, the voices garbled, and the whispering constant but indiscernible. Nearly half the people in our congregation left at once, and the cavernous sanctuary was left dotted with the fragments of community. Fabric samples were picked for the drapes that would cordon off the unused pews where our bustling church family once sat.

As an adult, I had conversations with my parents and learned just how much they protected me from at the time. I learned what had occurred when I was too young to know the details but old enough to feel the chaos in my body. The pastor had been grooming and sexually abusing women who went to him for pastoral counseling. When his actions were exposed, he admitted to other church leaders what had happened. Yet when it came time to tell the congregation why he was no longer the pastor, he changed his story and denied it all. For the women who survived the abuse and had to witness his reversal from private admission to public denial, it was undoubtedly horrific. The community began openly debating the truthfulness of the women's claims. Those enraged by the accusations were unaware that the sister, mother, or daughter sitting beside them in the pew had survived the trauma. Many members were simply unwilling to accept the truth of what had happened.

The horrors of clergy sexual abuse are profoundly complex; the fallout can take years to navigate and leave multiple layers of wounding. This is always the case when abuse happens at the hands of the people we trust, who are supposed to protect us and who represent a God who is all present, all knowing, all powerful. As I made sense of this story, the layers of wounding were never in question for me. I see survivors of sexual abuse in my practice all the time, including sexual abuse that occurred within the church. It makes me think of these women, whose names are still unknown to me but who I grieve with and for all the same.

It took me years to understand that the rest of the community faced a trauma of their own. The congregation was left with two opposing stories: one from church leaders telling them that their pastor had been sexually abusing women, the other from the pastor, who claimed he was being wrongfully accused. No matter what they believed, they lost some part of their security and their identity. Someone they trusted to care for their community, someone they trusted to tell the truth, had lied.

The pastor left, as did half the congregation who believed him. This included family members of the women who had been abused. Not long after he left, the pastor died, and he took with him any opportunity to know more about what had happened. What did not die with him was the legacy he left behind: the loss of trust, the covering up of sexualized violence, the trauma caused within the communal body. All of us were hurt by the unwillingness to name what really happened out loud and to heal the systemic wounds.

This story is painfully unoriginal and just one example of the insidious forms of abuse that can happen in spiritual communities, some of which occur more commonly but that are harder to name and point out as wrong because there are no laws that defend us from them. But we are getting better at naming what was previously unnamable. There are more spaces, better language, enhanced research, and an increased willingness to talk about what spiritual abuse and trauma mean and to find ways to heal from wounds that occur in communities of faith.

Our wounds, whatever they are, are made more powerful by the silence around them. The naming of what has hurt us, how we have hurt others, and how those hurts still linger is the very undoing of the cloak that keeps the pain unseen and unaddressed. And this—the naming, the unveiling, the unsettling—as painful as it is, is central to how we heal.

What Our Bodies Have Always Known

When I started thinking about this project, I did a search for existing academic literature on religious abuse and trauma. I reviewed all the articles unearthed by our most powerful search engines—anything with the words *spiritual trauma, spiritual abuse, religious abuse, religious trauma.* I found just over a hundred academic articles, about sixty book chapters, fifty dissertations, and twenty-four books. The earliest piece of literature was published in 1991. Researchers were catching wind of the need to study, theorize about, and write about ritual abuse, cults, and trauma that comes from abusive spiritual communities. Not long after my initial search, the number of published pieces started to climb.

The 1990s were not that long ago, and the dramatic increase in academic and theoretical discourse suggests we are gaining better language to define what spiritual trauma is, how it occurs, and what to do about it. Research and science are at the forefront in many fields of academic inquiry. I know from colleagues doing stem cell research, cognitive neuroscience, and biomedical engineering that there are treatments the public is as of yet unaware of coming for myriad illnesses and diseases. But in the social sciences, and psychology in particular, it seems academia is often the last to know what the bodies of people everywhere have been telling us for millennia.

Spiritual trauma didn't emerge in the 1990s, nor did it emerge when White evangelical Christians started talking about it. It has always been here. Spiritual trauma is the result of conversion therapy and what the queer community has faced in faith communities. Spiritual trauma was the outcome when parents of children with disabilities were told the disability existed because they sinned; when Indigenous children were taken from their families and placed in church-run residential schools; when clergy sexually abused children and the people in power hid it; when Christians owned slaves and used biblical proof texts to justify their tyranny; and when White Europeans, bolstered by colonization and the Doctrine of Discovery, stripped untold numbers of communities of their ancestral knowledge and spiritual traditions in the name of evangelism. Spiritual trauma has been with us for as long as religion has existed. Spiritual trauma has been with us for as long as people have used power to dominate others in the name of God. Spiritual trauma has been with us for as long as anyone has been told they were broken from the start.

The academic and clinical communities are just now catching up. Awareness allows us to name things, to put language to what bodies have always known and felt. This is part of how we heal.

I started speaking about spiritual trauma publicly when I was halfway through my doctoral degree. As a therapist, I have specialized in trauma: understanding it both theoretically and academically as well as working with it in my practice. It was in my practice, while treating clients with trauma, that I first started to hear stories about how the lines began to blur between their trauma and their spirituality.

In some cases, people came in with clear-cut stories of hurt. Someone had abused them and had done so in the name of God. Now they couldn't sleep at night, didn't want anything to do with God, would rather die than step foot in a church, and felt dissociative and detached from their body except for when they were panicking and in a state of terror.

But more often than not, I encountered people who had symptoms in the present that they could not trace back to anything in particular. After all, how do you pinpoint something that was woven into the very fabric of your development? How can you talk about a thing that hurt you when you were told that doing so would be a sin and would cause eternal suffering? How can you name a wound when the source of the trauma cut you off from knowing you were wounded in the first place?

As stories of spiritual trauma were coming out in therapy sessions, I began to reflect more on times when I had incurred hurt and—even more challenging for me—times when I was a part of hurting others. I set out to learn more, heal more, and help others do the same. This is a collection of things I have learned, things I am still trying to understand, and an acknowledgment of the voices who have guided me along the way.

I know that some of you reading are part of a church community, walking alongside others who have spiritual trauma or trying to navigate your own. Some of you reading have found that the only way to retain a sense of spirituality and relationship with God is to leave the communities and buildings that remind you of how you got hurt. And for some of you, the thing that has saved your life is getting as far away as possible from anything carrying a whiff of the religious or spiritual. I had all of you in mind as I pulled together this collection of ideas and conversations where you could be understood, heard, considered, valued, and treasured, regardless of what you believe, what you have experienced, or how you identify yourself.

To trust me to do that, you might want to know how I understand myself. I am a White, cisgender woman, an uninvited guest who has settled with my husband and daughter on land first occupied by the Coast Salish peoples. I have disabilities, but not ones that are visible. I am highly educated, trained as a psychologist, and I am within the broader community of folks who want to keep learning from the person of Jesus and how he lived in the world. I find that the word *Christian* means very different things to different people, and I am increasingly aware that for some the word itself is connected to trauma, so I use it sparingly, wanting to privilege the reality of the people who have been harmed by a legacy of in-group bias or a sense of rightness. Those who identify as Christian have a great responsibility to own the harm done to others in the name of God and to devote themselves to learning from and treasuring the people who have been called "other" by those with the most wealth, power, and control.

By learning together, I hope we can create conversations wide, gracious, patient, and informed enough to build communities of faith that hurt others less, that can acknowledge any hurt caused without ignoring or avoiding it, and that offer gentleness and healing for the people who belong to them or who associate with them. We will do this by talking about what spiritual trauma is, how it impacts us, and how we heal.

A word on reading: what I love about media in written form is that you can read all the way through a book a thousand times, or not at all, or start and stop and restart again, or decide it's not for you and never touch it again. In situations where there has been abuse and trauma, there has often been an imbalance of power and control. I want to remind you that you don't actually have to read this, that you have choice, and, should you wish to continue, that engaging with choice around this topic can be an act of healing, recovering a part of yourself that was previously disavowed.

What Is Spiritual Trauma?

A formal definition of spiritual trauma is still emerging. In the process of writing this book, I sought to learn as much as possible from people who knew a great deal about spiritual trauma, either through study or personal experience, and in some cases both. We'll hear more from them throughout this book.

One of the questions I asked as I was gathering information was "When you hear the words *spiritual trauma,* what comes to mind?" Here is what they told me.

> What came to mind for me was this image of trudging through mud. That's what spiritual trauma means for me. It's very hard to explain because it doesn't feel tangible like a lot of emotional hurt or abuse. It doesn't feel like you can necessarily grab ahold of it, but it feels just as real. (William Matthews III)

> Well, I know that it's pervasive. That's the first thing that comes to my mind. (Roberto Che Espinoza)

> Spiritual trauma cuts to the core of who we are. And it's just deep. It's not something to take lightly, you know? So that's the first thought I have: there's a little bit of fear and trembling, in a healthy way. (Alison Cook)

I just crossed my arms. So I'm going to go with what my body is doing. When I hear the words *spiritual trauma*, my heart instantly goes a little bit faster. And I crossed my arms, which is a bracing posture. So I think my body says this is something that is painful and damaging, and it has a physical response to it. (K.J. Ramsey)

It feels to me like there's this almost infinite distance between the words *spiritual* and *trauma*. One feels extremely raw and concrete, visceral, gritty, chaotic, and disorganized. The other feels ethereal, transcendent, open, not unembodied, but almost like super embodied, like spiraling upward. It almost feels like an oxymoron to put them together. It feels like dry water or something strange like that.

For that reason, too, I feel an instantaneous instinct to be suspicious of the idea, like how could this even be a category? There's an instinct toward minimizing, which I think is telling about some of the forces that gathered together to make this difficult to grapple with. Maybe that's why it's really important. (Preston Hill)

When you look back over the history of the church, you see the church has been complicit and initiated a lot of oppression and violence, and that has caused trauma in a lot of people. This is going back fourteen hundred years at least. (Mark Charles)

To better understand the complexity and nuance of spiritual trauma, I want to start with an introduction to trauma in a broader sense.

The first time I began to understand trauma conceptually, I was in a graduate-level counseling psychology class. My professor, psychologist Rick Bradshaw, defined trauma as the negative events and experiences that confuse us, overwhelm us, and leave us feeling powerless. As such, trauma is about what happens inside us—our inner brain-body response to what happens to us or around us. When we perceive threats or potential threats, mechanisms outside our conscious control get activated to help us respond and survive.

What we perceive as threats exist on a continuum. We all have daily stressors: someone cuts us off in traffic; we are running late for a meeting; we see a former love interest at the grocery story on the exact day we decide that dry shampoo and stained sweats are the right choice for the trip out, so we hide behind the chip display for five minutes. (That last one is strictly hypothetical, of course.) Most of us who live in cities, are in school, commute by car, have children, are renting housing, or are paying a mortgage have some baseline stress. It can wear on our bodies over time, but the stress is there to help us navigate these events and environments. In a perfect world, our stress is useful; we experience a stressor, feel the activation in our bodies, and that activation helps us create change, ask for help, perform at a high level, or ask others for support. We use up the energy, the stress goes away, our bodies recover, we can rest again, and the cycle repeats itself.

Then there is a next-level kind of stress. This stress feels like overwhelming terror, like something inside us is being gripped by the tight hand of fear. This stress comes from wondering if what is happening will obliterate us. The violation of our safety strips us of our agency and robs us of our ability to stop something or protect ourselves or others. These experiences of stress change us; categorically, they sit outside our ability to tolerate, cope, or manage them. We are particularly vulnerable, and the wounds are most catastrophic, when the trauma happens when we are young or at the hands of people who should have protected us.

When this happens, it's almost like a part of us becomes stuck in the moment. Whether we have the language for it or not, we are left feeling fragmented, disorganized, and with our sense of safety and presence shattered. Some parts of us continue on with life, and other parts of us continuing to live as if the trauma is still going on or could happen at any time. These parts of us, locked in the experience of the trauma, come with their own ways of protecting and defending us. Even as we grow and time passes, they live on, in a way frozen in time, reminding us of what happened and sometimes feels like it is still happening. Any number of things can cause us to feel this way—too many to name, really. But the result is that how we experience ourselves and the world is fundamentally altered.

One comparison of what is happening inside a traumatized person that comes to mind is a broken bone. The bone is still there, but now it is in pieces that create pain, dysfunction, and a new way of orienting to the world. On the outside, it looks like any other limb, but when we look at an x-ray, we see that what was once all connected has been fragmented. The proof of trauma is in the shards.

In this analogy, the shards are the symptoms we commonly associate with this kind of stress trauma, what we call "big-T trauma" or "shock trauma." Symptoms include constantly anticipating something threatening, avoiding or wanting to get away from the things that remind us of what happened, and memories coming to us unbidden. This sometimes happens in nightmares or flashbacks, when the body feels the same sensations it felt associated with the trauma. These can seem detached from what is actually happening around a person and often don't make sense logically. But the body is telling the story of harm that was done, desperate to be heard one way or another.

These unwanted reminders are like unpaid parking tickets that show up in the mail: bright yellow, hard to ignore, demanding our attention. They are there to say we have unfinished business; something that happened still feels alive in us.

We can also experience symptoms in how we feel day to day. Clinically, we call this "alterations in mood," but that is an oversimplification. In truth, we change in how we orient to the world and what we believe about ourselves, others, and the future. The foundation of the story we hold about ourselves gets disrupted. People experiencing this often feel wildly disoriented; nowhere feels safe, and not even the rest offered by sleep is accessible. Suicidality, self-harm, and substance use can appear as symptoms when we feel trapped and are looking for ways to alleviate this pain. We can even experience changes in our consciousness, leaving us feeling shut off, numb, or in a dreamlike state. The parts of our nervous system that pass messages between body sensation and thoughts get disrupted. The mind effectively floats away to somewhere safer than the horrors of whatever is happening in the present.

Our bodies know how to shut down, and they do so when there are no other pathways for enduring what would otherwise be unbearable. When it might mean annihilation if we move a muscle, when it might mean we cannot go on if we actually see and feel how awful the moment is, we can—totally unconsciously—disconnect from the present by collapsing, losing consciousness, or storing no memory of what is happening. When this occurs at the time of the traumatizing injury, it's like a switch gets flipped on that never gets flipped off. Unlike other symptoms, which are alarming and seemingly mismatched to the present, dissociation is like an invisibility cloak, even concealing its presence to its own host, which enfolds us in the absence of presence and the felt sense of disconnection from one's bodily self.

The big-T trauma and resulting distressing experiences get our attention. They are meant to. But they are not the only kind of trauma. Next to them on a continuum are the things that happen so frequently or so early in life that we formed no autobiographical memory of them, or they were so commonly occurring or normalized in our family or culture that they never seemed noteworthy. Instead of a single rupturing blow, there was a subtle contortion of ourselves into a posture we had to take to stay safe, to make us good, to keep us insulated from whatever we believed we needed to avoid. These chronic injuries can be psychological, relational, and spiritual. And without the obviousness of the big-T traumas, the little-t traumas leave us confused about why we are in so much pain. Culturally speaking, we rarely think of it as trauma at all. Because of our limited understanding, we believe trauma is the single awful thing that happened. When we cannot identify an event that explains why we feel so awful, so unlovable, so desperate for escape, we are plagued by guilt and shame and worthlessness, even without a narrative for why. Meanwhile, our bodies are telling the stories of the injuries we've incurred.

A Kind of Shattering

Philosopher Michelle Panchuk says the word *trauma* is "multiply ambiguous."[1] We use the word to mean what happened to us but also what happened to us *because* of the trauma—as well as a combination of the two. Increasingly, the word is colloquially and carelessly used to refer to experiences that are upsetting or unfortunate.

There are multiple clinical definitions of trauma. The most recent edition of the *Diagnostic and Statistical Manual for Mental Disorders* defines a traumatic experience as "exposure to an actual or threatened death, serious injury, or sexual violence."

Such an event is directly experienced or witnessed by a person, happens to someone they love, or is repeatedly encountered, as in the case of first responders and therapists.[2] This description seems to capture some of what is encapsulated in trauma, but it misses the impact of the event.

The Substance Abuse and Mental Health Services Administration in the United States defines trauma, in part, as the "lasting adverse effects on the individual's functioning and mental, physical, social, emotional, or spiritual well-being," and also as "the experience that is too much to handle within the body's normal coping mechanisms."[3] Judith Herman says it is any event that overwhelms a person and removes their sense of control, connection, and meaning.[4] Bessel van der Kolk says it is the imprint of pain, horror, and fear that lives inside a person because of what happened to them.[5] Trauma expert Peter Levine describes it this way: "Trauma is about loss of connection—to ourselves, to our bodies, to our families, to others, and to the world around us. This loss of connection is often hard to recognize, because it doesn't happen all at once. It can happen slowly, over time, and we adapt to these subtle changes sometimes without even noticing them."[6]

While specific diagnostic categories and labels are useful, defining trauma in terms of only the symptoms or the biology misses the very core and experiential fragmentation and alteration of meaning, personhood, and interconnection at the center of one's existence.

Trauma, in a word, is a kind of shattering.

The word *trauma* is Greek in origin and means "wound." This can help us re-engineer the definition. We can ask questions like What are the things that have wounded me? and What kinds of things wounded me in a way that left a lasting impact? The things that wound us fall into two categories: the things that happened to us and the things that *didn't* happen but should have. We are wounded by the bad things that happen to us but also, in the words of Gabor Maté, by the good things that didn't happen to us.[7]

You might want to pause and think about your own wounds that came from both commission and omission. Or you might want to come back to them at another time, as this is where things start to get a little more complicated. Sometimes the strategies we use to hide our woundedness from ourselves are sophisticated. They are outside our conscious awareness. The defenses we have put in place are well-entrenched, practiced over a lifetime, and reinforced by those around us. Often, there are more wounds than we're prepared to examine, especially if we have survived by pretending the wounds aren't there. We have strategies to keep ourselves from identifying what might be there if we just looked more closely. We stay busy, numb out, and avoid. We say to ourselves, "Just don't think about it," "Man up," "It wasn't that bad," or "They really did love me." As my mentor and colleague Saj Razvi once said, "People can build a beautiful life on top of a nightmare,"[8] or in the words of a beloved patient of mine, "Sometimes people turn a defense against pain into a denomination."

If that sounds complicated or far-fetched, let me give you an example.

I have lost track of the number of times a person has said to me in therapy, "I'm fine. I had a perfect childhood. But . . . can you help me with my alcohol abuse, or my rage at my partner, or the panic attacks I'm having at night? . . . But those are totally unrelated to my perfect childhood." The issues that bring people to therapy don't appear at random. But when we have never been supported to process what happened and how it impacted us then and lives in us still, we are forced to find ways to go on, protect ourselves, and exclude the painful memories and emotions from our narrative. We use defensive behaviors, thoughts, and processes to avoid facing what lives in the basement of our conscious awareness. We do that so much over time that these defenses become normative for us, and we become disconnected from the original injury. This process happens within our internal world, and it expands outward to the world around us. Our families, communities, and cultures—along with many of our traditions, practices, or lack thereof—are coated with the residue of trauma from this lifetime and times past.

This sounds bleak, and you might be thinking like many therapists do early on: trauma is EVERYWHERE! That's true, but healing, hope, and resilience are everywhere too. The potential for remaking ourselves is woven into our humanity. In a paradoxical way, trauma and healing are always woven together: the more we can begin to see the trauma in and around us, the more we can also begin to see healing, resilience, and beauty in and around us.

In sum, trauma is how what happened to us lingers in us. It is the big and little things that cause a fracture deep inside us and between us. It's the things that leave us caught in a cycle of pain, avoidance, and numbing. Sometimes the wound is so accepted, hidden under our defensive strategies, that we don't even know it is there, although some part of us senses something lurking in the shadows of our interior life. It's a kind of haunting.

There is one thing we do know for sure about trauma across a continuum: our bodies always tell the truth. Even if we find a way to cover up trauma, the story always comes out—if not in our thoughts or in our relationships, then always in our bodies.

Innate Longing for Connection

When I am giving a lecture or workshop about spiritual trauma, I normally run into some questions right around this part of the presentation. Questions like "But what does this all have to do with our church?" and "How long until you get to the part about God, or cults, or _____?"

This isn't surprising. We struggle to see spiritual trauma because it's interwoven with every aspect of our lives. Many of us have been taught that spirituality is somewhere else—that it's in the realm of the incorporeal, the transcendent—not connected to our bodies or our present. We've understood our mind and body are distinct from each other, and our body and the bodies of others are also separate, functioning in isolation and independently self-sufficient. We have come to believe our relationship to ourself is different from our relationships to others.

The separation of all parts of life is one of our original wounds. As a result, it's helpful to define spirituality here as connectedness and the search for meaning and the sacred. In one 2018 paper addressing psychiatry and mental health, the authors define spirituality as the guiding framework that helps a person address the deep, existential questions at the center of human life.[9] Psychologist Chuck Macknee suggests that spirituality is a core dimension of our humanity that nudges us to discover meaning and purpose and to connect with self, others, and God.[10] I have come to understand spirituality as an innate and fundamental orientation toward and longing for connection that is part of a reparative undertaking to mend the fragmentation within and among us and all living things. Religion is norms and traditions around spiritual practices engaged in by groups of people looking to find answers to spiritual questions and longings.

Spirituality is often seen as outside what is happening right now—in this body, this brain, and this beating heart. But neuroscientific data proves that the drive for connection is wired into our bodies from birth. We have reflexes and automatic nervous system processes that are geared up from the moment we're born to help us locate our caregivers (through sight, sound, and smell), reach toward them, interpret their emotional states, and seek closeness and comfort.

The longing for connection is in each of us from the beginning. It seems as though everything we thought lived *out there* in the spiritual realm is *right here*, in our material bodies. And everything in our material bodies is telling a spiritual story.

As we come to see that spirituality is about connection, it becomes clear why there is no spiritual trauma that is not also physical, relational, and psychological. And it goes the other way too: no physical, psychological, sexual, or relational trauma leaves our spirituality untouched. Trauma of any kind strikes to the core of who we are, and yet through its signature hints at the way that we can never be completely shattered. We can never fully disconnect mind from body or body from mind, even if we have been lead to believe we can, even if it feels like we can, even if we wish we could. No part of us is left untouched by spiritual trauma.

We are and have always been integrated, whole beings. It isn't possible to create hierarchies of what kind of trauma is the worst, but we do know that when trauma is interpersonal and occurs early in our development, it impacts our minds, nervous systems, beliefs, and relationships in profound ways.

Imagine a person who had a safe and connected upbringing: one in which they were told they are good, are surrounded by people they can trust, and have witnessed others be supported as they heal in various ways. Then say that person gets into a car accident. The road to recovery may be long and painful, and there still may be lasting psychological injuries to attend to for some time, but that is all happening within a social context where people agree the car accident did indeed happen and mutually agree that it was awful. That person's recovery is supported and affirmed.

In contrast, consider the person who is told horrible things about themselves and the world and the future on a loop starting at an early age by people who were supposed to care for and protect them. That in itself is awful and would undoubtedly have a lasting impact. But then consider this person being praised and celebrated as they grew up for believing all the horrible things they heard, and as a result passing along all these negative ideas to others.

I wanted to make this point right here because there is something particularly insidious about spiritual trauma; it is almost always relational, often occurs at a young age, may happen over long periods, and is normative, ignored, and sometimes framed as a great good. Even if the word *God* or *religion* was seemingly never involved in the abuse, these early experiences of feeling unsafe fundamentally alter how a person navigates the world and their disposition toward meaning and connection. This too is spiritual trauma.

But spiritual trauma can happen in more direct and explicit ways. It has been said that people are meaning-making beings. When considering the neuroscience of development and trauma, I suggest that another statement for understanding spiritual trauma is that we are *association-making* beings. Our brains and nervous systems are making associations all the time. We are unconsciously learning and remembering, for example, that dessert tastes good, that fire is hot and we need to keep our distance, and that if we are thirsty and drink water we will feel better. Our minds make associations regarding things that hurt us or are scary even faster and more effectively. So if we experience a scary or painful event, our brains will categorize it—and anything involved with it or like it—as potentially harmful.

In her book *Sacred Wounds*, Teresa Pasquale defines spiritual or religious trauma as "any painful experience perpetrated by family, friends, community members, or institutions inside of a religion."[11] Marlene Winell, author of *Leaving the Fold*, developed the term *Religious Trauma Syndrome* in 2011 and suggests that religious trauma is the physical, spiritual, psychological, and emotional damage that comes from being indoctrinated into an authoritarian religious community and then subsequently leaving it.[12] Significant and specific trauma occurs among those who leave their faith community. This is especially true when faith teaching and community belonging are interwoven with conformity and obedience.

Yet people can experience religious trauma and still stay within their religion. In addition, spiritual religious trauma can occur at the hands of an authority in a community that does not identify as religious. A coach might abuse a child who had prayed earlier that day for God to watch over and protect them. Or an older sibling might abuse a younger sibling and say, "If you were better behaved, God wouldn't have allowed this." It may not be obvious to an outsider, but for the survivor, the trauma is connected to religion in some way, as the event and religion are linked in their memory.

Another term to consider is adverse religious experience (ARE), which includes any religious belief, practice, or system that undermines a person's safety, autonomy, or agency and negatively impacts their physical, social, emotional, relational, or psychological well-being.[13] These experiences include abuse or neglect at the individual level as well as practices that affect communities. This definition of ARE feels close to the definitions of trauma given above, highlighting the many ways a wound can show itself in different facets of our lives. Some of these adverse experiences happen in isolation, such as a single incident with a leader, or they may take place when someone is visiting a community they are not tied to in an ongoing way. But as with other forms of complex trauma, our religion often keeps us connected to systems, communities, and relationships as a primary value yet also at times serves as a mechanism of control. As a result, it's more common that AREs happen repeatedly, at multiple levels, and in a variety of ways. In his book *Done*, Daryl Van Tongeren says spiritual or religious trauma "occurs when people who are in vulnerable situations and seeking help are wronged or exploited in the name of or through religious means or ends."[14]

Michelle Panchuk's description of spiritual trauma shows how it can occur either within or outside religion. She makes the following points. First, the trauma is caused by something that the person closely associates with religion or spirituality, is inflicted by someone who is thought to be a stand in for the Divine, is said to be justified by the spiritual practice or religious beliefs, or occurs because of religious or spiritual practice. For example, a pastor who uses Scripture to justify a public humiliation, a rabbi who is sexually abusive, a venerated leader in a yoga community who touches students inappropriately under the guise of education, or a parent who physically abuses a child and says they are disciplining in a biblical way. Second, the survivor believes that spirituality or religion was somehow the cause for what happened. Last, the post-traumatic psychobiological responses are connected to God, religion, or spirituality in some way.[15]

Here's what I like about Panchuk's definition: (1) the trauma can be a wound of many kinds, (2) there is no specifier about severity, (3) it allows for traumas of omission and commission, (4) the person doesn't necessarily have to articulate it was a trauma, (5) they don't have to be leaving their religion or spiritual practice for it to be valid, and (6) the responses can be expressed in any domain of the human experience.

In environments where individuals lack information—particularly about trauma, mental health, and abuse of power—having clear definitions with specific and definable criteria can be empowering. Living through and after trauma can feel more like a nightmare than any list suggests. For that reason, I think the words of J.S. Park capture the experience of living with the legacy of spiritual trauma poignantly: "If my body is a house, then spiritual trauma means that my house is haunted and that God is the ghost."[16]

For many of us, the house is haunted.

The Spiritual Dimensions of Trauma

In 2023, Heidi Ellis and colleagues published a paper titled "Religious/Spiritual Abuse and Psychological and Spiritual Functioning."[17] The authors present evidence of how religious and spiritual abuse and trauma have identifiable mental health outcomes, which can include risky sexual behavior, disordered eating, self-injury, anxiety, depression, substance use, and other trauma-related symptoms. But it can be challenging to separate religious and spiritual trauma from other kinds of trauma.

In a study of 308 individuals who had a history of religious and spiritual trauma, the individuals were asked about their spiritual and mental health struggles and their traumatic experiences. Using statistical analysis, the researchers identified the ways in which religious and spiritual trauma uniquely affected people's psychological and spiritual functioning. They found that religious and spiritual trauma is indeed a measurable form of trauma that can greatly impact a survivor's mental health and spiritual functioning—inflicting wounds that strike to their core. The more frequent the incidents of trauma, the more severe the symptoms. Because spirituality and religion are central to a person's identity and are expressed in community, injuries of this nature are both deeply existential and deeply relational. How individuals view themselves, their world, and their future and how they make meaning are all impacted.

Even if trauma happens outside a religious context, it changes our spirituality. It shatters the assumptive worldview we had before we were hurt. It reinforces the fear or mistrust that characterizes being profoundly overwhelmed and existentially wounded.

Here is an example. If I walk through life believing each chair I sit on will hold me up, but then one day I sit on a chair that crumbles under me, my assumptions about chairs will change. I'll likely approach other chairs with more caution, inspect them before sitting, and be reluctant to let the full weight of my body rest on the chair. The chair is like our spiritual worldview: we don't think much about how it is supporting us until it stops doing so. Regardless of the nature of trauma, all forms erode meaning and trust; undermine self-worth, value, and humanity; and can increase guilt, shame, and fear. In response, we develop defensive and dissociative strategies to protect ourselves.

Several trauma experts underscore the spiritual dimensions of trauma. Bessel van der Kolk describes trauma as "a hole in the soul."[18] Resmaa Menakem describes intergenerational trauma as a soul wound.[19] Robert J. Lifton argues that trauma changes a person's sense of human connectedness in a way that dislodges the self.[20] Judith Herman purports that the foundation of faith is basic trust, which is first learned in primary relationships, and that trauma fractures this trust.[21] Darryl W. Stephens notes, "Fundamental self-worth, human connection, and basic trust are deeply spiritual issues."[22]

In their paper titled "I Will Never Know the Person Who I Could Have Become," Scott Easton and colleagues reveal that survivors of clergy sexual abuse have found that it touches every aspect of their lives.[23] But even when the trauma happens outside a faith or religious context, the spiritual self is impacted profoundly.

One 2017 study examined how adverse childhood experiences (ACEs) impact spiritual struggles and mental health later in life. Researchers found that adults who survived ACEs grappled with faith and spirituality as adults, even when the ACE didn't occur in a faith context. Further, the extent to which they struggle with religion and spirituality was found to be an important link between trauma exposure and the development of post-traumatic stress disorder.[24]

It is important to note that religious and spiritual struggles occur when a person's religious or spiritual belief or practice leads to negative thoughts or emotions and conflict or distress. We do our best to catch these wounds by identifying what our bodies say to us in the aftermath. Again, if each part of us is connected—our past, present, and future; our minds, bodies, spirituality, and relationships—there will certainly be places of pain that bleed across the artificial lines we draw. While it's helpful, for a time, to identify where the wound began, we ought not to assume the wound stayed in that place. All that does is ignore the pieces of shrapnel hiding out in other parts of our humanity.

◆ ◆ ◆

When I was starting to think about spiritual trauma, I one day found myself lying on the rug in my living room. It had rained that morning, and the droplets of water combined with the light coming in the kitchen window cast a prism of colors across the wall. The light came in through the window from one direction but seemed to bend and bounce across the room, splitting into all the colors of the rainbow.

Rainbows from a prism typically represent jovial whimsy, magic, hopeful possibility, and even pride. They seem categorically different from the imagery I described earlier of pain-ful injuries, shrapnel, and broken bones. Still, trauma, like light, has a specific point of entry. Yet even if trauma happens in one domain, it is connected to all the facets of the human experience. No matter the point or manner of entry, a trauma impacts each part of our lives, each dimension of our human experiences.

Perhaps I'm stretching the analogy, but if you'll allow me, trauma is like light in another way: it helps us see what is there. It shows us where the places of injury are inside us—the places that we have learned to turn our gaze away from—while also highlighting the patterns, people, and systems that caused the wounding. It allows us to see the places where healing is needed outside us so others don't get hurt like we did.

• PRACTICE •
Locating Ourselves as Bodies Here and Now

After reading this chapter, you might have noticed your body communicating through loud sensation about memories of past injuries. Or you might have noticed you forgot all about yourself as a body, or your body went numb or seemed to disappear altogether. Reading about distressing things can pull us out of the present moment and drop us back into memories associated with distress. To end this chapter, or really any time while reading that you need to support yourself as a body to be here and now, not then and there, try this practice.

Allow yourself to visually scan what is around you right now: What do you see? What catches your eye? How is the light hitting the different objects? What is behind you?

Allow yourself to notice what your body is touching right now. This could be your feet on the floor, your body supported by a chair, or your hands holding this book. What about the boundaries of your skin? Can you feel where your clothing is touching your body? Notice how the air feels on your skin.

Allow yourself to travel inward, noticing the sensations within your body. You might become aware of your internal temperature, pressures on your organs (if you are full, need to use the bathroom, or feel the tightness of your clothes on your body), or energy moving through you (up and down, in or out, and front to back).

If you are able to do so, place your hands on your body and remind yourself of the date, how old you are, and where you are. Thank yourself for being here, now.

Mihee Kim-Kort and K.J. Ramsey
on Defining Spiritual Trauma

I am eager to introduce you to Mihee Kim-Kort. Mihee is currently pastoring a church in Annapolis, Maryland, and is a doctoral student in religious studies at Indiana University. This means she likely had a million papers she could have been writing or reading, or people she could have been talking to, if she wasn't talking to me about spiritual trauma. She has important things to say about queerness, race, and Asian American feminist theology and is the author of *Outside the Lines* and *Paper Cranes*. Even though we come from different disciplines, I once heard her describe herself as a hope-monger, and I knew immediately I would find myself at home in the presence of her words. Here is a snippet of our conversation.

Mihee

When I hear the words *spiritual trauma*, I think about manipulation. When I think about the Korean immigrant churches that many folks like me have grown up in, no matter what denomination, they tended to have a bit of evangelical flavor, and that makes sense because of the history of American missionaries going abroad. Korean churches (in Korea and the US) were influenced by both Protestant and Catholic missionaries—as well as evangelical ones, like Billy Graham.

And even if they came from specific denominations, you had to speak a certain way and carry yourself a certain way and hold certain ideals. The Korean culture that was present at the time tended to be very traditional and expected certain gender roles and held certain expectations, depending on how old you were and what generation you were in.

Looking back, it seems a little benign. It didn't feel terribly oppressive or like brainwashing; it felt like just the structure of our community. It was just the way that we related to one another. We knew our places; we knew where we could speak and how to act. But I look back to a few moments here and there, where you see some of the cracks, the system breaks down in certain places. As I got older, I didn't see women doing very much except in the kitchen—serving and cleaning. Sometimes they would be allowed to pray from the lectern. It wasn't until college that I discovered that in my denomination women could be ordained to be elders and pastors.

My dad went to seminary later in life, while I was starting college, and he told me about being in class with female students who were pursuing ordination. And I was like, "What are you talking about?" I remember arguing with him about how the Bible says this, and women are supposed to hold this role. I think of spiritual trauma as how you internalize something so much that you don't even realize the sort of self-oppression it produces. *Insidious* is a really good word for it. It becomes an atmosphere and climate you don't really notice, but you know that you can't live without it in some ways. That was our only community growing up.

It's the kind of thing where it feels like you just can't trust yourself or know yourself. It's the kind of shaping and constructing disciplining that happens so that you don't even really know your own voice is gone until you've left the community and have had a chance to look back.

I have to say, there are really important and wonderful and significant things there. In these systems, they aren't ever just one thing. But what anchored that community was a very specific idea about what was proper and acceptable, about what was pure and good. And that was all the stuff around a certain kind of sexuality, a certain sort of identity, a certain kind of masculinity or femininity: it was very rigid. There was just no room for any other kind of thinking.

❖ ❖ ❖

Meet K.J. Ramsey, a therapist who writes about faith, psychology, and living with chronic illness. Her writing is equal parts incisive truth-telling and poetic psychoeducation, and I trust her completely. Her second book, *The Lord Is My Courage*, is about her journey through spiritual trauma and redefining faith and finding healing on the other side. When we sat down together to talk about spiritual trauma, I asked her to start by telling me what happened for her when she heard the words *spiritual trauma*, and here is what she said.

K.J.

I just crossed my arms. So I'm going to go with what my body is doing. When I hear the words *spiritual trauma*, my heart instantly goes a little bit faster. I crossed my arms, which is like a bracing posture. So I think my body says this is something that is painful and damaging, and it has a physical response to it.

I am a survivor of spiritual trauma: what I often refer to more as religious trauma with spiritual abuse and also long-term exposure to high-control, high-demand religion. And so as a person re-covering myself, those are loaded terms that are attached to very painful stretches of my life, and painful responses that I've had in my own body as a result of being silenced and shamed and diminished as a person. As a therapist, I work with so many people working through this, and I think of their faces and their bodies and the confusion that they have experienced from being part of spiritual systems and relationships where their full selves are not honored and protected.

There were layers of uncovering what was traumatic, through naming spiritual abuse and the resulting trauma in my own body and in my husband's body. There was also this uncovering of a lineage of spiritual trauma of my childhood, but also family of origin and the way that spirituality has been passed down through generations. So there are multiple layers there.

My husband was a pastor at a church where I also ran my therapy practice. And we were controlled and diminished by a very domineering leader. The rest of the staff was treated so terribly behind closed doors and in staff meetings. Seeing the response when people would speak up about something feeling off, we began to notice how diminished we were. It was the cries of our own bodies and souls of overwhelm and deep, deep sorrow and sadness and physical illness that made us pay attention, and we started to just reflect: Why is church so messed up? And why does this feel so messed up?

The first person who started to give us language for what was happening was Diane Langberg. But it was really in the aftermath of leaving, when I started to uncover more of my own symptoms of post-traumatic stress, that I had to take what my body was saying seriously and really listen more closely. So that's the beginning of an answer. I had to come to this through a very personal experience rather than as a clinician, which I think is probably true for a lot of us.

One of the most damning and destructive parts of spiritual trauma is the way that the diminishment of humanness is handed down as spiritual maturity. And it's actually more a perpetuation of dominance and control than love. Our spiritual communities and spiritual practices are more a manifestation of control, uncertainty, and upholding a power structure than being fully human. There is a deep mistrust of the very things that would tell us something is wrong, because we've been taught that not listening is actually holy.

[As our conversation went on, K.J. shared a piece from her book *The Lord Is My Courage*.]

Silence can soothe us and silence can scar us. I was raised for reverence, to sit still and silent in church, and to give people in leadership, especially men, unquestioning respect and honor for their "God-given" authority. I learned to raise my voice when grace amazed me but relegate it into silence when harm alarmed me.

Silence is the arbiter of scarcity, the force of coercion and control that those who hold the most power wield to maintain the status quo. If power can only be held in the hands of a few, then pleasing them is what buys us belonging. So we learn to fold our hands and cross our legs and put a smile across our faces to hide our hearts' frown, all the while absorbing the bad, bad news that God is actually a power who must be pleased and love is just a reality we receive when we are good enough.

I was taught reverence for the sound of a preacher's voice and the pages of my Bible, but I was never taught to reverence the sounds of my own body and soul.[25]

TWO

Shards of Glass

One evening in 2022, I was greasing a baking dish before filling it with brownie batter. I pushed hard into the corners of the dish and felt a sharp, hot flash of pain in the tip of my middle finger. Blood pooled in the dish. I rushed over to the sink, the blood dribbling down my finger and across the floor. As I held my open palm under the cold running stream, the water cleared away the blood enough that I could see there was a shard of glass sticking out about an eighth of an inch. I had no idea how the glass got into the dish, but it was now in my finger.

I was able to grab it with my other hand and pull it out. Then I had a glimpse, the briefest flicker, of more glass buried in my finger. I kept the wound under the stream of water, hoping the bleeding would stop and I would be able to get a better look at it. I poked and prodded, and eventually I called my mom and some medically knowledgeable friends. They reassured me that the glass would come out on its own. When the bleeding slowed, I could not see anything, so I put a Band-Aid on my finger and went to bed.

In the following days, I soaked my finger in hot, salty water numerous times. Gradually, the cut started to heal. I was glad it didn't get infected, but I was frustrated and aggravated by the constant irritation that I could do nothing to resolve. I would have done anything—including cutting my finger back open—to get the buried shard out if I didn't have some very smart people reminding me this likely wouldn't go well. I knew the glass was in there but couldn't get to it—and it was extraordinarily painful.

In the coming weeks, every time I touched something with my right middle fingertip—car keys, keyboard, forks, water bottle, my own hair—it felt like my flesh was getting sliced open again. Yet at this point it looked like a perfectly healthy finger. If someone inspected it and knew the story, they could detect a small lump deep under the surface of my skin. Something was definitely there, but it was invisible if you didn't know to look for it.

Months passed, and I began to notice changes in the way I did things. I held a pen differently when writing. I held my hand differently when typing to avoid the pain. I also began to wonder if there was really anything in there. The mound on the end of my finger had flattened. As I thought back to the flicker I saw after pulling the first piece of glass out, I wondered, *Did I really see anything else?* Maybe there wasn't a shard in there after all, and this was simply my body's reaction to all the poking and prodding I had done to get out a piece of glass that was never actually there.

Then, midsummer, a small lump started to form about half an inch below where the glass had originally gone in. It was painful to the touch, felt dense, and looked slightly red. Why was it showing up in a different place? As summer went on, the mound seemed to grow a little each day, and eventually in September it looked like a little mountain. It was more painful than ever, and I would often unconsciously touch it while doing other things, pressing the sides, trying to encourage it along. Then, on a Friday in late September when we were on vacation as a family, it opened at the top and watery fluid started to leak out.

(Thought you were reading a book about spiritual trauma instead of an essay about a minor finger injury? Hang in there.)

The next day I was reading my daughter a book in the backseat of a rental car as we cruised down a freeway, and of course I was also low-key pressing the sides of this finger mountain—almost out of habit by this point—when the glass suddenly poked through. I yelped. There it was: half out of my finger and half in. My husband found a place to stop the car and pulled the shard the rest of the way out. It was so much bigger than I would have ever guessed—yet somehow also smaller than it had felt or seemed. We took ceremonial photos with the shard placed next to various objects to give a sense of the scale, as one does, and shared them with everyone we knew. All said, the shard was in my finger for nine months, minus a day.

A few weeks later, I started to make connections between my experience and spiritual trauma. My finger injury has much to illuminate about the injuries people experience that fester for so long that they seem like they are normal. Even if the injury was so long ago we can barely remember it, something really did happen, and it hurt us. Something that was never supposed to be in us—a story, a belief, an ache, a fear— got lodged inside and changed our way of being.

No matter how much we try to convince ourselves otherwise, how familiar the injury becomes, or how much our community ignores it, our bodies know the truth of what hurt us.

Our bodies will keep telling us that something is not right. And because our brain-body systems are oriented toward health, that something will get pushed to the surface, even if it has been buried so long that we forgot it was there.

My memory of seeing that tiny speck of glass helped me to understand what was happening and why. It was like a foothold for all those months when I was in pain—a coherent, easily identifiable *why*. I could say, "Of course it hurts. There is a sharp and dangerous foreign object in my finger, and my body is constantly communicating that the object is hurting me and needs to come out."

In the previous chapter, I noted that knowledge alone doesn't heal trauma, but it does minimize the shame and fear that are caused by not knowing. Knowing can also prompt us to show compassion to ourselves, to ask for what is needed, and to articulate to others the source of the wound. When we know that something is there and where it came from, we can also begin to ask, "What does this need to heal?" Maybe we don't know, but we might seek out someone who does.

The Second Arrow

What if, instead of seeking out help and healing, I had blamed myself for the entire predicament? *If I had been paying closer attention while greasing that dish, the glass wouldn't have gotten lodged in my finger to begin with.* Sometimes knowing comes with judgment, if that is the eye we've been trained to see ourselves with. Self-blame is often referred to as the second arrow. The chronic pain recovery community talks about this principle a lot, as it is common with disability, injury, and illness.

Imagine that I am going through life and get injured. I twist my ankle playing tennis with a friend, or I scrape my leg working in the garden, or I burn my hand on the stove. The initial wound is the first arrow. It happens in the course of being human and moving around in the world. But then I start to tell myself a story about the wound. Maybe I start to shame myself or beat myself up for doing that activity in a specific way. That is the second arrow. It's curious how we sometimes add more pain to our pain. Perhaps we think that if we're hard enough on ourselves then we won't do that thing that hurt us again; we'll get the message and change our ways.

Why do we do that? If no other strategies for understanding pain have been modeled for us, the second arrow gets internalized. When we were younger, perhaps our families or people in our communities responded to pain with judgment and shame. In some circumstances, our pain may have even been called "sin." Based on what we learned firsthand and saw around us, our default is to judge and criticize.

It's harder than we might think to uproot the internal narratives we have collected from families or faith communities that doled out judgment and punishment. But it can be a gift to ourselves not to place another arrow in the bow. Instead, we can say, "No wonder I'm judging myself. This is what was modeled to me, and even celebrated, for all those years." Instead of shooting the second arrow, we need to realize that the place of pain left by the original arrow needs protective healing and gentle attention. It needs something different from what caused the pain in the first place. It needs love.

Back to the piece of glass. What if it wasn't just one shard but hundreds of tiny fragments embedded under my skin? And what if they were buried under there so early that I didn't remember each of them? And what if people told me that the tiny pieces of glass were a good thing, that the pain would fix what was wrong with me?

Imagine a community of people inflicting harm on a child and then telling them this way of behaving is for the best,

43

until the child grows up and no longer feels their body at all. The numbing protects them from feeling the pain as they go about their day.

When we think about our emotions, our social and psychological selves, our spirituality, we can see how used to these kinds of injuries we are. Our consciousness about trauma and what is abusive is expanding, but there is still much harm that is done to people emotionally, psychologically, and spiritually—in the name of tradition, in the name of discipline, in the name of God.

The Symptoms of Spiritual Trauma

I find it fascinating that while I had the shard in my finger, I subtly shifted how I did things in order to minimize the pain. I altered how I typed, held a pen, opened the car door, and turned the key in the ignition. If there had been multiple pieces of glass in my fingers, you can imagine that what had already started to happen to me would have accelerated.

We intuit how to avoid the things that hurt us. We find other ways to carry on, but when those adaptations are unnatural, unsustainable, or unsupported, they can end up creating more injuries in the long run.

When I was experiencing back pain, I saw a movement specialist who helped me identify how the pain was compounded because the muscles in my left glute were tight, which was misaligning my pelvis. How did my glute get so tight on one side? When I ran, one of my feet wasn't hitting the ground flat because of an old knee injury. Our bodies have workarounds to manage pain, but they don't eliminate the pain. In fact, some adjustments eventually cause their own pain.

When we're living with trauma, including spiritual trauma, we develop adaptations to work around the pain. Perhaps we were highly controlled, and so we do not speak up or out against rigid rules. Perhaps we were told from a young age that we will burn alive for eternity if we are not good enough, not spiritual enough, and so we try to pray in the perfect way. Perhaps we are highly sexualized and then blamed for how anyone objectifies us, and so we learn to blame ourselves too, hating and punishing our body for being bad. Perhaps we were told we are bad and unlovable and need to be rescued from ourselves, and so we defer all responsibility to others who seem good, lovable, and provide a clear path for our salvation.

Trauma is like pieces of glass lodged in our nervous systems. Our bodies, our very psyches, will start to tell the story of all the ways we've been hurt, even if we still have a story floating around in our minds—as a kind of learned helplessness—that this is good and how it should be. Symptoms of spiritual trauma can show up in our physical bodies, our behaviors, our emotions, our thought life, and our spirituality. They are, after all, connected. As we have already discussed, spiritual trauma can be a single event or a series of interrelated and often relationally experienced traumas that occur over time, also known as complex trauma.

As a means of highlighting just how far the shards of glass can travel, here are some examples of the ways this pain can show up in our lives.

Psychological Symptoms
- Internal chaos, confusion, or disorganization: feeling afraid and anxious all the time
- Superstitious thinking and behavior: wondering whether we will be punished if we do the wrong thing, or anticipating severe consequences for making the wrong choice or upsetting someone

- Flashbacks or nightmares: unintended remembering of events that were scary, stressful, or unresolved and feeling agitated or dissociated because of it
- A lack of identity or a sense of wants, goals, and values: not knowing who we are or feeling confused about who we should be
- Difficulty with identifying and feeling emotions: finding it difficult to feel feelings from the inside out
- Difficulty making choices: feeling paralyzed by options or ruminating on what could go wrong with each choice
- Boundary challenges or confusion: finding it difficult to set boundaries with others, not knowing what boundaries with friends or leaders are appropriate, and having difficulty with appropriate sharing with or caring for others
- Anxiety or panic, feeling on edge: feeling agitated in the body, like being hooked up to an electrical current, or having chronically tense muscles
- Chronic, neurotic, or misplaced guilt: wondering if we made the wrong choice or hurt someone, or anticipating that we likely will
- Ongoing and pervasive shame: feeling broken, unlovable, unworthy, or deserving of bad things, even in the face of relationships or experiences that prove otherwise
- Anger, rage, and defensiveness: experiencing reactivity, flying off the handle, explosive and disproportionate reactions, and reluctance to take responsibility
- Hopelessness, helplessness, or despair: feeling powerless and unable to change future or present

circumstances and believing no other reality is possible

- Depression, emptiness, and loneliness: feeling empty inside, isolated even if others are around, unreachable, lethargic, depleted, and overwhelmed at the prospect of change
- Self-harm: hurting ourselves in any way, depriving ourselves of rest, food, or other bodily needs, or punishing ourselves through creating pain
- Suicidality: wondering if it would be better to be gone or planning to end our life
- Grief and profound sadness or loss: experiencing seemingly unchanging heartache and emotional pain, or the sense of having a hole inside
- Difficulty feeling joy, pleasure, or peace: experiencing little or no effect even when doing things that used to feel enjoyable or feel pleasurable to others
- Perfectionistic tendencies: setting rigid expectations for self or others related to thinking, behavior, interactions, or value systems, and consequences if something isn't perceived as perfect
- Hatred or shame of one's body, sexuality, and physical needs or limitations: having unrealistic body narratives in which normal challenges, emotions, sensations, or behaviors are considered disgusting or awful
- Difficulty with self-responsibility, self-care, or self-love: experiencing difficulty owning our own actions and choices, and nurturing the self through actions or thoughts
- Difficulty enjoying sexual pleasure: experiencing genital pain, fear of sexual arousal or desire, resistance to

sexual relationships, or shame about sexual desires and behaviors
- Risky sexual behaviors or sexual activity
- Inability to trust others and anticipation of rejection: feeling suspicious of others' motives or keeping ourselves at a distance to avoid judgment
- Immense guilt if not helping others or caring for others: feeling the pressure to save, convert, or rescue
- Skin picking (dermatillomania) or hair pulling (trichotillomania): experiencing distress before the behavior and relief after engaging in it
- Substance use or addiction to other processes or behaviors: using drugs, alcohol, food, pornography, or certain behaviors (shopping, gambling, etc.) to manage pain or distress or feel feelings, even if negative consequences are involved
- Eating disorders: having a preoccupation with clean eating, compulsive eating, food restriction and avoidance, eating and purging after (through vomiting or exercise), and eating things that are inedible or harmful to eat

Physical Symptoms
- Chronic fatigue
- Autoimmune disorders
- Chronic pain
- Sleeplessness or oversleeping
- Lack of appetite or binge eating
- Frequent illness or injury, or impaired healing
- Chest pain or gastroenterological issues and irritable bowels
- Inability to notice or identify body sensation or pain

Social-Relational Symptoms

- Loss of community connection and broader social support
- Rejection and social isolation
- Restricted social networks
- Relationship conflict or stressors
- Family conflict and stressors or loss
- Damage to one's social self
- Social anxiety

Spiritual symptoms can also appear. When a person's spiritual system has been the core of who they believe themselves to be—the most important, most enduring, most true part of their identity—spiritual injuries and wounds can leave a person without a sense of who they are. They might feel left without a meaning-making system, a clear sense of reality, the comfort of ritual to navigate life transitions or difficult experiences, the comfort of certainty, and the shared narrative and language through which to form connections and community with ease. Our assumptions about the world are shattered in a way that existentially makes it difficult for us to feel the ground steady under our feet.

Spiritual Symptoms

- Deconstruction of or de-identification with one's religious or spiritual background or traditions
- Fear, vigilance, dissociation, avoidance, or acute emotional reactivity when in the presence of reminders of the past religious or spiritual background
- Negative or fear-based beliefs about one's own relationship with God or one's sense of self-worth

- Difficulty with moral discernment without guidance from an authority figure or mistrust of oneself
- Anger at God or at religion or spiritual practices in general

Whenever we are presented with a list of symptoms or defining diagnostic criteria, it's important to be aware of three specific points. First, a list of symptoms doesn't really capture the way that people are dynamic, can adapt, and have their own stories. Problems can be rattled off like they are a grocery list, but it is profoundly terrifying to experience a panic attack, especially when it happens in a formerly peaceful place or in response to something that used to feel safe. A list can't convey the devastation of a person feeling like they are bad, awful, and unlovable at their core.

Second, we should consider multifinality and equifinality. *Multifinality* means "many ends." Some folks who have a similar kind of trauma can end up experiencing very different effects. One person has panic attacks, another experiences addiction, and so on. Multiple responses can all spring from the same root cause. *Equifinality* has the opposite meaning: different experiences that result in people experiencing similar effects. An example is when people who have lived through different experiences all end up experiencing depression. This helps us remember that many different outcomes and expressions of trauma can exist at the same time.

Third, although symptoms exist as phenomena all on their own and can often drive people to seek treatment or identify the need for care, they are listed as symptoms because they are the downstream effect of something else. They are a form of communication that our bodies are using to send us a message. To understand them, we often need to look deeper.

What Freud Knew

This is the perfect time to tell you a story about Sigmund Freud. Feel free to pause a moment here to chuckle, shake your fist, or get out a highlighter, depending on how you feel about his theories. But there's good reason to look at his work here, and it's likely not what you think.

Freud, who was originally a neurologist, is the founder of "the talking cure"—as psychotherapy was originally called. As a result, the field of mental health owes a lot to his work. Freud introduced us to the unconscious: the ways there can be things going on inside us, driving us, that we are unaware of. At a time when so much of the world still centered on the thinking, conscious, rational mind, his insights into the unconscious were ahead of their time. But not many people know Freud has a connection to the field of trauma.

Around the turn of the nineteenth century, when Freud was developing his theories and practice, he was treating the daughters of several Austrian aristocrats for hysteria (a whole other book could be dedicated to the problems with this term). In Western Europe, hysteria was considered a medical illness experienced exclusively by women. It was characterized by anxiety, disorganized sexual behavior, insomnia, emotional dysregulation, fainting, relational conflict, and alterations in mood. It was difficult to treat and confounding to experts. As Freud started to work with these women, they began to remember and disclose experiences of sexual trauma, often with family members, frequently their fathers. Freud believed them, and his theory of trauma was born. In his opinion, hysteria was the way his patients' bodies communicated about the sexual trauma, especially when their minds—and the people they were in relationship with—prevented them from naming the truth.

To paint a clear picture: Freud realized that these untreatable symptoms were arising from sexual abuse perpetrated by the men who were giving him a job.

As Freud's biographers tell the story, he presented his theory at a meeting of aristocrats, many of them his colleagues and fathers of his patients.[1] Accepting his theory would have required these men to admit what they had done to their daughters, or to accept what had been done to these young women by the men within their circle. Unsurprisingly, they reacted negatively, and Freud succumbed to their pressure to adapt his theory. This emergent knowledge about how trauma manifested in the bodies of women was suppressed—that is, until the trauma to men following the world wars and the Vietnam War became too significant to ignore. Only then did a definition of trauma and its effects on the brain-body system reemerge.

In a letter from 1897, Freud expresses "surprise that in all cases, the *father*. . . had to be accused of being perverse" if he were to attribute hysteria to sexual abuse, "whereas surely such widespread perversions against children are not very probable."[2] In writing this, Freud exhibited a tendency he spoke of elsewhere in his theories. When the reality of what happened is profoundly disturbing, we are capable of pretending it did not happen at all. He called this "the defense mechanism of denial."

Before he set his theory aside, however, Freud's insights on trauma were as close to our current theories as you could imagine. For example, he identified these characteristics of trauma:

- Trauma does not disappear, even if we don't talk about it—and *especially* if we don't talk about it. It lives in our bodies and keeps reappearing.

- Trauma comes with a physical and emotional charge, and that charge needs to be released from the body for us to heal. This is why things come back to us over and over in the form of our fears and nightmares and hauntings; it is our bodies playing it all out again.
- When we can't or don't release the physical and emotional charge, the trauma creates what is called "a strangulated effect": the normal discharge of emotion is repressed, stuck in the body, and causes symptoms like anxiety, pain, and illness.[3]

Freud was wrong about a lot of things, but he was right that the stories of our trauma need to be told. Our bodies need to know we are safe so that we can move forward without our coping strategies overwhelming us to the point where we are damaged not only by the initial trauma but also by how we try to manage the pain of it.

How Our Bodies Remember Trauma

In the many decades since Freud, we have come to understand the imprint of trauma on the body to live in somatic memory (or body-based memory), changing a person's biological stress response system. We now understand that the adage "It's all in your head" is scientifically incorrect. Nothing "in our heads" isn't also in our bodies. When something happens that overwhelms or scares us, our brain-body systems activate a particular series of responses to help us stay safe. First, we look for help and ask for help, assess the danger around us, or protest. The ability to look to outside connections for solutions to our distress or to communicate "I don't like this" or "This doesn't feel good" or "I need help" is wired into us from birth. We don't have to learn how to do that; we just learn more sophisticated ways of articulating what is wrong as we grow up.

But if that doesn't work or endangers us further, our brain-body circuitry tries another response. It activates the major muscles and accelerates heart rate, changing our field of vision and perception of sound, among other things, to help us physically defend ourselves or get away. In this state we are mobilized, prepared to respond to or flee from threat. If that doesn't work, or the stress is overwhelming and there is no way out, our systems shut down. Our bodies instinctively know how to preserve energy, decrease threat, and live in a kind of non-real, pseudo-alive state that can range from depression and hopelessness to overwhelming fatigue and semiconsciousness, where a person does not even notice or feel sensation at all.

When these states of overwhelm or nervous system activation occur, before the body moves toward a total shutdown, everything going on around and inside us gets locked into a specific kind of nonverbal memory. The activated or mobilized nervous system states get associated (or paired) with a place, smells, sounds, body posture, time of day, time of year, who is around, what we're feeling inside, even what happened before and what happened after. Sometimes we can remember it and talk about it, such as when a specific awful thing happened that had a distinct before and after.

But when the situations creating the overwhelm are normalized, even celebrated, and happen in places where we want to belong and stay safe relationally, it's hard for us to know that we are storing memories of trauma that are shaping our personality structure. Sometimes we can't remember the overwhelming moment because we were so young that our brain hadn't started storing autobiographical memory yet. Instead, we just have these imprints of overwhelming fear, or we have a horrible feeling that we are fundamentally broken or flawed and unworthy of love. When someone has experienced harm at such an early age that they don't remember the details, the result is that the shame, aloneness, and fear can get woven into their sense of identity so intimately that it is hard to believe this is a trauma response and not just the truth about who they are as a person.

Our bodies are so good at trying to protect us from what once hurt us that when something reminds us of the trauma, we sometimes react as if we are experiencing the threat again. It's as if we are back in the moment of the frightening event just by thinking about it or by encountering those same smells, sights, postures, time of day, words, or other contextual cues. A key feature of trauma is that these sensations, memories, and activations get locked into place. It is as if a switch gets turned on as we rush down the stairs in the middle of night after hearing a loud noise, and the switch never gets turned off. Traumas, by definition, dissolve the neatly arranged ideas we have about time; they blur the categories of the past, present, and future. The pain and terror of the past are alive in our nervous system in the present as we anticipate future distress.

As psychiatrist and trauma expert Bessel van der Kolk has noted, the stress of these overwhelming and traumatic events create long-term reminders of what happened, which are associated with chronic changes in the body's stress response system and alterations in memory.[4] This ongoing state of heightened alert changes the way our stress hormones are released and alters how we perceive the sensations in and around us. Traumatic memories can't be integrated and processed the same way as other memories. They leave people feeling like they are constantly reliving the past.

In *The Body Bears the Burden*, neurologist Robert Scaer highlights how unprocessed trauma changes the nervous system, the brain, and our physiology. He notes that "the most common complaint in current medical practice, that of persistent and unexplained chronic pain, has its roots in the actual changes in brain circuitry associated with unresolved trauma."[5] Therapist Natasha Files has argued something similar: "The moment we sweep a feeling under the rug, we sweep it right into our nervous systems."[6] The stuff we do not feel does not disappear. Our bodies, in their wisdom, keep track of unprocessed trauma so that when the time is right, when we can't wait any longer, or when we finally feel safe enough to look at it all, we have the opportunity to feel what has gone unfelt. Our feelings of an event or experience need to be felt in order for us to heal; this is true whether the event was recent or in the distant past. As overwhelming as it can be when the bodies we were taught to ignore or silence or mistrust demand our attention, our need to allow our emotions to be felt and released is as natural as a wild animal's instinct to shake after an attack. It is as natural as the trees dropping their leaves in the fall or the shoots springing up from the ground in the spring. We were taught to fear facing the intensity of emotion and sensation in our bodies, but that doesn't mean doing so is dangerous or bad.

We might blame our nervous system or a sensitive or overactive gut or whatever physical symptom we experience, seeing it as proof that our bodies are bad the way we may have been told that they were bad, or that they are leading us astray from objective truth. But our bodies are telling the truth. Our bodies—bless our flesh and blood—say what we have been unable to say, what our voices and thoughts have been trained not to articulate. The story our bodies are telling is sometimes about right now, sometimes about what we've been through, and sometimes about what has happened to those in our family systems. But the story always, always, deserves to be heard.

It is not a betrayal but rather a prophetic word to the systems or people who have done harm.

This is part of why labeling trauma a disorder is a misnomer. When we say that something is a disorder, it can imply that the person is the one with the problem. Trauma experts know this is not true; when someone experiences trauma, it is the community and the context that are disordered. The person, by way of their nervous system response, is just doing what socialized humans do when they experience a scary, overwhelming situation and can't discharge the fear that gets stirred up in their body or stop it from happening again. Physical symptoms can be understood as the body's instinctual drive toward restoration. They are not proof of any lack of faith, weakness, or badness. Rather, they are nature's imprint within us, our bodies' effort to process and complete what is unfinished and living on—in us and through us.

Brain imaging research shows that social-emotional hurt activates the same areas of the brain as physical injuries.[7] Conversely, when others help us, it can be the foundation for our healing. Right from the get-go, when things were scary for us, our bodies knew how to look around to see who was there and who could help. Our orienting reflex activated the muscles in our necks and eyes to turn toward our caregivers. The hardwired drive for connection was there to help us find safety and security in the face of distress.

People are much less likely to experience the enduring impact of trauma if, before and after a traumatic event, they are part of a community that acknowledges and affirms their bodily response when they are afraid and helps them find their way back to relational and physical safety.

A field of study known as epigenetics examines how trauma alters gene expression, and research affirms that the impact of trauma can go on for generations. Even if the initial trauma happened to a single person, if their communities or customs for creating safety were inaccessible, the person's genetic material could change, and therefore the effects of trauma could be passed on to those who came after. Our cultural perception that a disorder lives in or belongs to individuals highlights the long-lasting legacy of colonization and our view of ourselves as more separate from each other than we are. As much as we have learned to think otherwise, we are collectively interconnected with those who have come before, those who are around us now, and those who will come after us.

Information Is Healing

The process of healing trauma is something we will give much time to in this book. But it cannot be overstated that information about trauma is *itself* healing. In communities of faith where information about science, psychology, or mental health is unavailable, withheld, or portrayed as threatening, people are often left without the tools to understand their experiences. When discussing religious trauma, philosopher Michelle Panchuk has called this "hermeneutical injustice."[8] When we lack understanding about what's happening, we struggle to identify why we feel so awful inside or to identify the source of the injury as coming from abusive systems, beliefs, or leaders.

When we feel awful, the only explanation in the minds of many for why we feel awful is that we are awful—the echo of the anthem from many faith communities ringing in our ears. If we had tried harder, had more faith, prayed more, or said the prayer correctly, we wouldn't feel this way. Our anxiety, shame, or self-hatred is used as proof that we need saving, that we are bad, that we can't trust ourselves. Not understanding what has happened to us, which can lead to self-blame, is part of how the problems in these systems continue. Thus, understanding itself can be part of healing.

Knowledge can be so empowering that some leaders and systems intentionally disparage or restrict access to psychology and science as a means to keep people powerless. Leaders may fear that access to this information will threaten their own authority and that they will lose their influence, that those under their authority will see through the systems and leave. This is not so different from how some religious and spiritual contexts require the swallowing of one's voice: individuals are not allowed to question what happened or what is happening. Being able to tell one's story and use one's voice can help us to begin to mend the fragmentation and reclaim agency, making visible what was made invisible so that healing can take place.

Learning about traumatic stress exposes the lies we as a society tell ourselves about how okay we are, how rational we are, how independent we are. The neurobiology of traumatic stress and its healing is particularly elegant and hauntingly poetic. Although from the inside trauma feels chaotic and disorganized, our bodies really have so much order to them. And what we need to heal is surprisingly simple. As Judith Herman has asserted, trauma by its nature is unspeakable, yet it demands to be told.[9] Trauma demands to be seen to be healed, to be held in community so that we can know the aloneness and terror of the overwhelm is over.

We will explore this more in upcoming chapters, but for now I want to reiterate how adaptable we humans are. It is amazing what we can get used to with enough exposure. As a species, we can learn to believe anything is normal, including harm, especially when it is also somehow connected to our needs, like belonging and relationship. We can be so easily drawn to systems that harm us when they feel familiar, when they remind us of where we've come from, or—here is the tricky one—when they promise to rescue us from those patterns we've been steeped in but are just the same system with better branding and a music team.

✦ ✦ ✦

Back to the shard story for one last round of analysis.

When I had glass in my finger, I did normal things that everyone around me was doing, but they were extraordinarily painful. When I brushed my teeth, picked up a utensil, or drove a car, if anything touched my finger, it hurt in a way that fingers without glass in them wouldn't have hurt. The cause of the pain was buried within my fingertip. No one touching my hand could have guessed that they were activating a pain response.

When there is a trauma living unprocessed in us, we learn to work around it in our daily lives, but it hurts. You might have heard this referred to as a "trigger"; I like to think of it as an activation of the autonomic nervous system. We hurt not because we are incurring a new injury but because an existing wound gets touched. Our body responds to the pain from the old wound to remind us there is something that needs healing and attention. But we need our present awareness to remind us that the pain we're feeling is a kind of remembering, a signal about what we have been through, as opposed to the present moment being a threat to our well-being.

When we have spiritual trauma, the shard of glass might get bumped by key religious or cultural phrases or patterns of speech, religious buildings, reading religious texts, being around people who were part of our religious or spiritual experience, or, if you haven't yet put this together, reading a book about spiritual trauma. This might be one of the things that touches the place of pain. The way we know those places of pain exist often comes through the body: we get hot or tight, or feel terror or fear or rage, or freeze or blank out. Or we might feel as if we are back where the hurt happened, almost as if we get transported across time back into the moment of injury. Those are not just symptoms of the body's remembering of spiritual trauma; they are the ways the body reminds us of unprocessed pain and inner wounding—no matter the source. All of this is the body's good and instinctual way of telling us, "Something here still hurts and needs to be attended to." That might be a very different story than the one you received about your body being bad and untrustworthy. If that is the case, and it seems near impossible to believe, you might begin by asking, "What if it is true?"

The places of hurt and how we respond are different for everyone. Remembering this helps us feel compassion and curiosity instead of offering judgment, shame, and blame. My writing about this might feel energizing for you; you may finally be understanding some things about someone you love or why something that is painful for you creates no re-action for anyone else. Or you might be experiencing a flood of fear, and it is hard to keep reading. All these reactions make sense as part of the human experience in general, but they also speak of who you are as a person and what you've lived through.

Most important to remember is that the glass eventually worked its way out. My bodily system, in its wisdom, knew the way to get something that didn't belong inside me out. When the glass was nearing the surface in those last few days, my finger was hot, red, swollen, weeping fluid, and painful, even when I wasn't touching it. It reminded me that healing can be gentle and graceful and slow, and other times painful, intense, and uncomfortable. At times it takes courage to stay with the process and let our system travel the road toward wholeness. As we keep moving forward in this conversation about spiritual trauma, I want to remind you that just as hurt can take many forms, healing can take many forms as well.

Even when it's hard, attending to our trauma through integration and processing serves our growth and healing. Even if we have memorized a story that our bodies can't be trusted, our nervous systems know the way to wholeness; it has been written into us from the beginning.

· PRACTICE ·
Body Gratitude

Through understanding trauma symptoms as the body's way of communicating about distress that is still living inside us, we have a new chance to listen and respond. To end this chapter, or any time you want to respond to the way your body is communicating in the form of symptoms, try the following practice.

Allow your hands to meet and, if you're able to, create friction and heat by rubbing them together vigorously.

After doing this for a minute, place your hands somewhere on your body, perhaps directly on the site of the activation, symptom, or communication. Take a moment to notice what kind of touch you can tolerate or what feels soothing or supportive—practicing with different forms of pressure or movement. Alternatively, if it is more comfortable, you might let your hands rest somewhere neutral.

Remembering how much choice you have with how you are in contact with yourself right now, you might imagine your hands extending care, gratitude, and comfort to the rest of your body in the same way you might extend your care through your hands to someone you love and want to nurture. As you extend care through your hands, notice if words come to your mind that speak directly to the nerves around the shards of glass in your own body. Perhaps it is as simple and profound as "thank you." Or maybe these thoughts are more conversational. If you need a sample script of what to say, try this one:

> You are saying so much, and you deserve to be heard. I want to listen and get to know the story you're telling me, even if that takes some time, even if it's hard to hear. Thank you for speaking up about what hurts, especially in a world that so often wants to shut this down.

J.S. Park on Fear-Based Spiritual Trauma

I want to introduce you to my friend Joon. You might know him online as J.S. Park, the Korean American hospital chaplain and author whose voice in the often turbulent land of social media is like a refuge, his storytelling like an elixir that somehow warms and thaws the frozen places in us that cause us to see each other and ourselves as objects or as problems to be solved. His voice and work are a lighthouse in the land of social media, and his book, *As Long as You Need: Permission to Grieve*, is essential reading. Here are some of his thoughts from a conversation we had about spiritual trauma.

Joon

I come at this from both an Eastern and a Western upbringing. I have a hybrid comprehension of what spiritual trauma looks like. I think the Western sense of trauma is very much like a clinical definition of how a virus affects a computer. And I like that definition. But when I look at it from the Eastern perspective of spiritual trauma, I think of the feeling of being cursed—that somehow there's a sentence on my life and that my own value due to other moral decisions I've made, or my standing in the community, or what I appear to be in my family and in my name, has wrought something on me that is irreversibly and irrevocably not repairable.

And so when I thought about spiritual trauma, even more so than the feeling of having a virus affect our wires and wares, I thought, if my body is a house, then spiritual trauma means that my house is haunted and that God is the ghost. And it's that feeling of being cursed. I don't have it in me to perform this exorcism, to get this sense that God hates me and is haunting me, to get that out and to heal that part of me. And I think that can happen certainly from bad theology and bad leaders. And in bad leaders, we're thinking in institutional and systemic terms, and of the forces that enable perpetuation of those abuses.

With my patients, they're in the hospital because of this physical illness. And at the same time, the spiritual trauma adds a layer of difficulty to their healing, because it is essentially telling the story of what their illness is all about, in relation to God and their own moral and spiritual value. I had a patient who said, "My pastor said if I get mad at God, I'm going to hell." Now that sort of spiritual trauma is a narrative that's going to get that patient stuck. It's not going to make them any freer or more liberated. And their anger, which I believe is justified and is right, has no place to go. And it seems to just make them sicker. And they seem to almost believe, one, that this disease was wrought upon me somehow because of the supernatural order of things, I somehow attracted it to myself, and then, two, that I have to just accept it because I am afraid to get mad at God.

That sense that God punishes, that God has cursed our lives, is a very prevalent narrative when it comes to spiritual trauma. And I think church leaders will use that for control and coercion. Leaders will use that to keep their congregation almost constrained. Because if you can sell fear in a church, you can also sell the solution to that fear, right? And church leaders, whether it's for the money or for their fame or for their reputation or for their congregation size, they're going to use those supernatural narratives and impose that superstition on their congregation in order to continually keep them coming back.

And so I think for those who are spiritually traumatized, it's like if I can fill up my fear meter, then I am right with God. Or if I can fill up my guilt meter, then God and I have good standing. And it's like, okay, I'm going to get my bucket of guilt and then we're okay.

And I chuckled because, on the one hand, it's like a knowing laughter because this fearmongering was used on me for so long. On the other hand, it's trauma laughter because it's so sad, and it's still ongoing and it's perpetuated. Most of all, I think of that feeling of being haunted, as if somehow God is after me.

THREE

Pulling Back the Curtain

A client walked into my office in a huff. Before even sitting down, he blurted out, "I have to tell you about my dream." Then he leaned forward and told me about what had come to him the night before.

Having grown up in a family that expected nothing less than perfection, this man originally came to therapy because he was burned out in his successful career, which he had pursued and excelled at because he was told it was his calling. He had become the very version of himself that he was told would be the most righteous and the most satisfying. But now, in his early fifties, he felt disconnected from any sense of vitality or self-knowing. During our sessions, he would regularly say that his ability to feel, to know what he wanted, was removed from him at a young age. If any shred of feeling and self-knowing was still there, he hypothesized, it was buried underneath all the things he had learned to believe and do to be like everyone else in his family and community. He had covered himself with so many layers of protection to guard himself from what was so very bad inside him that any trace of his true self was beyond his reach.

Typically, when we worked together, it seemed like his presence was a few feet back behind his body. He appeared subdued, flat, or what he called "the well-behaved boy." But today he was energized—literally on the edge of his seat.

He shared that in his dream he was pushed up against a brick wall, held there by a hand pressed right against his throat. The hand was disembodied, the wrist seemingly disappearing into total blackness. His feet were off the ground, and he couldn't get away or fight back. He was terrified.

Then his attention shifted to the hand. It was squeezing his neck so tightly that he thought it might kill him. But as he kept his attention on the hand and his gaze followed the straining fingers up to the wrist, he saw that the wrist slipped back behind a black velvet curtain. He had a spark of inspiration. Even though he wasn't strong enough just yet to wrestle out of the grip of the tightly clasped hand, he could bring his arms up in front of him and part the curtain. His fingers skirted the edge of the curtain, and the hand squeezed tighter. He felt terror rush through his body: Would it kill him to look? Would it kill him not to look? The sense of urgency mobilized him, and all at once he grabbed the curtain and pulled it open. Behind it was a complex series of machinery—levers and pullies and hardware that seemed to hold the hand in place, including a large red on/off button just within his reach. He looked to his left and right, and he saw others held up against the wall as well, their feet always a little bit off the ground. They too were held up by machines that all seemed to look and work the same.

As he strained to reach the red button, he woke up.

What Leads to Spiritual Trauma

As we've established, trauma is what is living inside us as a result of what happened to us. But what experiences contribute to the development of trauma? What kinds of things happen that can so profoundly wound us? We know that some experiences are more likely than others to create a traumatic imprint. When the experiences happen over and over again, across time and groups of people, we can see how they are not just single experiences but rather patterns, cycles, and systems.

Generally speaking, we are better at identifying singular horrific events that are likely to create a profound and traumatic imprint than we are at identifying dynamics, cycles, and patterns that commonly occur at a systemic level, including in spiritual contexts and systems. This is especially true when we are accustomed to them or they are culturally sanctioned. It can be challenging to see that we are living in a cycle when one of the functions of the cycle is to disconnect us from the internal strategies (embodied knowing and critical thinking), social connections, and resources that would highlight the abuse that is happening.

Common factors have been identified in a clinical and scholarly way as more likely to cause spiritual and religious trauma. When they occur together or to a high degree within a religious or spiritual context, we can identify them as religious or spiritual abuse. As with other forms of abuse, these patterns can be broken down into smaller units of behaviors, interactions, or practices enacted by a single person or by an entire community of people. However, it is when these specific behaviors, interactions, or practices happen in an ongoing way that they form a pattern of abuse. Repeated exposure to abusive patterns can simultaneously erode a person's sense of self and cause their internal processes to adapt to them, making it difficult to see or feel the harm that is occurring and do anything about it.

In what follows, I summarize these common factors using words that begin with the letter *c* to create coherence in explaining how the process unfolds. These are not perfect descriptors, but the common factors that contribute to spiritual trauma are control, consequences, compliance, codependence, and culture.

Control

At the center of abusive systems is control. The power is enacted in a top-down manner, as a means of maintaining control, while controlling others is also a means of accruing power. The power can be self-appointed or conferred by someone else, but in these systems power is used to restrain, coerce, or exploit others.

The control can be exercised or gained in a number of ways. Many of these behaviors can seem normal; you might look at the list of controlling behaviors below and think, *What's the problem with that one?* or *That doesn't seem so bad.* But when they are applied together over time, they erodes a person's sense of agency and their capacity to stay connected to their own power and choice.

Therapeutic models can help us better understand how abuse happens in systems and relationships. The Duluth Power and Control Wheel is often used in consciousness-raising and recovery groups to help survivors build awareness.[1] Religious trauma expert Laura Anderson has adapted this model to underscore the specific ways that power and control show up in religious environments. In her model, she highlights how power and control are exercised through loss of autonomy, isolation, minimizing/denying/blaming, emotional abuse, spiritual abuse, threats/accusations/intimidation, economic control, and sexuality/gender hierarchies.[2] (These are all themes that will show up in the various *c*'s listed and explained below.)

Here are some examples of how control is enacted.

Interpersonal or Social Control

- Cutting off relationships with others outside the group
- Limiting the kinds of information people have access to, especially if it challenges the thinking of or control/power held by the leaders
- Creating a strong in-group bias that renders those in the out-group as bad
- Creating demands on time and community commitments that limit contact with out-groups

Financial Control

- Requiring a portion of income go to the religious group
- Expecting people to volunteer excessively, even if doing so negatively affects other areas of their lives
- Limiting women's access to education or employment
- Guilting or pressuring individuals to give even more money to the community and suggesting that in return all their needs will be provided for (by God or by the community)

Physical and Behavioral Control

- Suppressing sexuality when not within the boundaries of heterosexual marriage
- Defining and policing expressions of sexuality in general
- Creating strict expectations about dress
- Creating moral superiority around categories of food and eating behaviors
- Holding expectations about leisure activities, including what can be read or watched, and shaming and devaluing behavior that is not "like the group"

Psychological Control

- Shaming and devaluing development of or connection to the self, and communicating that the self (and self-trust or knowing) is bad or sinful
- Forbidding critical thinking and encouraging self-policing of thoughts and emotions
- Suppressing of emotion outside worship experiences
- Praising blind faith while discouraging critical thinking or questioning
- Making decisions for individuals about career choices, dating and marriage, or hobbies/giftings
- Requiring giving authority for one's life to the leaders
- Promoting black-and-white thinking

Toxic and abusive religious or spiritual systems are often called "cults" or "high-control groups," based on the defining feature of extreme and rigid control that dictates group belonging. The term *high-control group* will be used throughout this book in regard to forms of spiritual or religious trauma that are connected to a group-based setting or a system that features abusive use of control.

Consequences

When individuals seek to break away from tight control, they can expect to face consequences—whether threatened or realized. The prospect of being punished ensures the individuals stay and don't threaten the power of the leader or system again.

Given how central wishing to belong is to our sense of well-being, in addition to the assumption that we are part of a chosen or special community, consequences often center on the loss of belonging. Consequences can include rejection by the community, public or private shaming, shunning, or the threat of eternal conscious torment in hell. When a person works for the group, whether in a paid or volunteer capacity, their position may be changed, their pay may be decreased, or they may face the loss of close ties with others. A person may also be required to engage in specific tasks as punishment, such as spending extra time under the tutelage of the leader or engaging in specific spiritual practices (e.g., extended prayer).

Occasionally, leaders in the spiritual or religious community will deliver punishments and tell the person that they brought these negative consequences on themselves—a form of victim blaming—and that this is what has to happen to keep the person and the community from more harm. In some cases, this is called "church discipline." The consequences are often felt in the body of the person as a downstream effect of what they have come to believe they did wrong. When this happens, the person internalizes the blame. Eventually, no one needs to be there to tell them what they did wrong; they blame and shame themselves all on their own.

Compliance

The fear and pain of consequences are enough to keep people compliant, even if compliance is not an explicit community value. Feeling the threat that comes with stepping outside the rules, people might even believe they are choosing to go along with the community expectations.

For example, if someone grew up being very afraid of hell, later they might gravitate toward opportunities they believe will help them to avoid it, such as giving money, volunteering their time, and memorizing sacred texts. They might believe each morning when they do their daily Scripture memorization that it is entirely their choice and not connected to deeply ingrained threats of eternal separation from God. In some cases, people may be praised, celebrated, and rewarded for how compliant they are, making them even more motivated to adhere to the expectations and standards of the community. The agony of consequences together with the reward for compliance can powerfully shape a person's behavior in spiritually abusive systems.

Compliance can be powerful for creating a sense of belonging. As the adage goes, we go along to get along. But the cost is agency: the sense of a robust, intact self with opinions, intuition, and autonomy. People may be told that the self is undesirable and that to be spiritually mature—and thus respected in the community and safe for eternity—they must "die to self," distancing themselves from any thought, behavior, or person that might draw them away from adherence to the way of being expected of them.

In some situations, compliance can become the seed of mental health distress, and clinical presentations of rigidity, perfectionism, and compulsions around required behaviors may begin to emerge. People might adopt speech patterns and behaviors that reflect what is idealized in the community, and they might become so fearful of being noncompliant that they begin to doubt their own judgment, questioning their perception of experiences or reality.

Whether or not it manifests in clinically acute ways, and no matter the cause, the belief that a person is bad, untrustworthy, and broken at their core is one of the most destructive things a person can be told or can come to believe. In many faith communities and belief systems, this idea of being unworthy is so reinforced that it does not register as foundationally destructive or a feature of psychological abuse. Telling people they are broken at their core is a sure way to create people who feel broken at their core. Feeling bad, wrong, or fractured at the core of who we are is a defining feature of spiritual trauma.

Codependence

When leaders have power and demand total allegiance from those in their sphere of influence, those under their control lose the ability to trust themselves, causing them to become codependent on the leader, community, or system. This codependence shows itself in a diminished sense of self, the giving away of personal power—in some cases disavowing one's rights and agency and voice—and the giving away of trust. People may look to someone else for approval, may be unable to make decisions on their own, may be unable to feel their own feelings, and may not be able to trust themselves.

One of the hallmarks of codependence is the sense that "I'm okay only if you're okay." The person's sense of self has become enmeshed with another person's. Their psychological stability is dependent on the other person's actions and mood. This can often lead someone to give the other person excessive energy, time, and resources, with the assumption that doing so will help the other person's well-being or rescue them from stressors, even if this is ineffective and becomes a continuous loop of self-giving. Often, this happens under the guise of helping, but in actuality this can be a means by which the helper gleans value and a place to direct their energy in lieu of tending to their own needs.

In the case of spiritual codependency, a person's sense of self has become so eroded, even demonized, that they give themselves over to the person or system they believe can save or rescue them. This creates a dynamic in which the person needs the beliefs, person, or system on which they are dependent; on the flip side, the system or abuser needs the person to stay in their pattern of dysfunction. The abuser or abusive system needs to teach people that their inner compass is faulty and dangerous in order to keep them under their influence.

Theologian and therapist Preston Hill (who we'll hear more from in the interview at the end of this chapter) has identified the process that keeps spiritual codependency in play. In his language, it is maintained through "spiritual gaslighting" and "learned spiritual helplessness."[3] Because people have been taught they can't make their own moral decisions, they learn to outsource their discernment to others—often a spiritual authority. This is learned spiritual helplessness. Hill says this is reinforced through spiritual gaslighting, in which anytime a person has a moral intuition about something or engages in authentic self-expression, exploration, or autonomy, the expression of the self is suppressed. When a person mistrusts their own discernment, they revert to the spiritually or morally sanctioned default. As a result, a person may be perceived as spiritually mature (as defined by those who have the outsourced spiritual authority, of course) when in reality they lack psychological maturity.

Culture

Imagine abuse is happening at an individual level. A church leader is sexually abusing a congregant or a group leader is shaming a community member. Why are experiences like this tolerated for so long? How can interactions escalate from what seem to be normal encounters to a person being trapped in a cycle and unable to leave or think for themselves? And further, how does a person with power get to the point where they can manipulate a large group of people? There has to be a culture that allows, condones, dismisses, or works to hide abusive behavior.

Imagine drawing a circle around two individuals. The culture is the people around them. Culture also includes the beliefs of the community about accountability, support, and expectations for leaders as well as who is valuable, who has a voice, and how that voice is expressed over time. Here, you might imagine the small circle nested within a series of larger concentric circles, and if you know anything about ecological systems theory, this image might be familiar. Here it would be worth spending some time considering how our environment influences us.

Everything Is Connected

Everything in life is a series of interrelated systems, so that shifts on large, systemic scales (like what is happening in the world right now, in the twenty-first century) can filter down to impact things on really small scales (like the cellular activity in my body as I'm writing this). When we see how all the systems we are a part of are overlapping, we can begin to understand how they impact each other. This helps explain how patterns of abuse can be reflected in so many different areas. They are echoes of the same wounds showing up at different levels and realms of how we move through the world.

Let me back up. If you are new to ecological systems theory, I want to introduce you to the work of Urie Bronfenbrenner. As a developmental psychologist working in the 1970s, Bronfenbrenner posited a theory about how our development is connected to the systems we live in.[4] For some of you, that might sound obvious, but for many of us this is a new way of thinking about the self.

If we were raised in an individualistic culture, it can be confusing and disorienting—as well as enlightening—to learn that the way we feel about ourselves was influenced by our context. Our context can be divided into five concentric circles surrounding us (see fig. 3.1). It can be paradigm-shifting to realize that the reason we even think of ourselves as individuals is the result of our context. If we were born to different parents, in a different culture, at a different time, we would have a very different way of understanding me, you, and we.

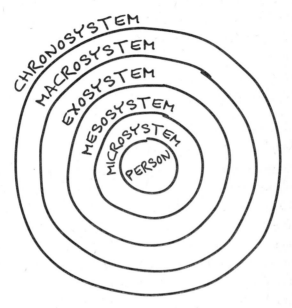

Figure 3.1. The Contexts That Shape Us

The first circle surrounding the individual is the *microsystem*. This includes the institutions immediately surrounding a person, like their family, school, friends, and religious community. Then comes the *mesosystem*, which consists of the interconnection between those in the microsystem, like how a kid's teachers and parents interact, or how someone's friends at church interact with their family. The *exosystem* is the social setting, which includes things like social services, media, local politics, and neighbors. A person's development could be impacted by how the removal of a social service creates stress in the family and impacts the person's quality of life. The *macrosystem* is the overarching culture and its attitudes and ideologies. These change from generation to generation and include values and the identities required for shared membership in a culture. All these concentric circles are situated within the fifth and largest circle, the *chronosystem*. This includes environmental events, sociohistorical circumstances, and the major shifts in a person's life that can change everything—such as a birth, a death, or a big-T trauma.

Bronfenbrenner's theory was first used to understand child psychological development. But we know that development happens in every moment across the lifespan and is impacted on a regular basis by the systems we are embedded in. Trauma, regardless of when it happens in our development, shapes how we come to experience ourselves. Since psychology has historically overfocused on the individual and their cerebral and intrapsychic reality, trauma has been understood to exist within the person. That is how I defined it earlier: it is not the thing that happened but our physiological response to it. That is a part of it, for sure, but that highlights the White, individualistic way of thinking about identity that has resulted from Western European thought, androcentrism, and colonization.

What this way of viewing the world and ourselves misses, according to ecological systems theory, is that our bodies exist in context and that our trauma was allowed to happen because of systemic factors. In addition, our healing—or difficulty healing—is also rooted in these larger systems. It is influenced by who has power, how much connection we have, the skills of the people we are connected to, and how we are or are not protected through it all.

In trauma language, these are the pre-, peri-, and posttraumatic factors: what happened before, during, and after a trauma. (We'll discuss these factors more in chap. 4.) We can sort these into the five concentric circles of the ecological systems theory. Ideally, the systems support our development, but that's not always the case, particularly when it comes to being in environments that are abusive or have a lot of dysfunction and chaos.

Picture the smallest circle of the figure to be our own body. That is situated in a system, within another system, within another system that is devaluating of certain kinds of people and sees the earth as a thing to use. It would make sense that those high-level beliefs would trickle down, showing up differently but reinforced within each smaller circle, until we have the experience of implicitly judging others and the automatic behaviors that lead us to abuse the earth without even thinking about it.

Why It's Hard to Leave Abusive Systems

I have heard countless stories of people who left an abusive church only to find themselves in a different one. Or they walked away from a cult only to discover that they accepted a job with a boss who had the same characteristics as the cult leader. Ecological systems theory allows us to see how patterns within abusive systems are replicated so readily in various contexts.

The parallels between family, development, and faith communities are not hard to draw, as high-control religious communities often use the language of "family" to exploit trust and engender a closeness and a kinship that haven't been earned. Although this isn't always the case, in some of these environments saying "we are a family" is one way to manipulate people into relationships where they are relegated to subordinate roles and are expected to follow paternalistic leaders.

Sociologist Nancy Nason-Clark has researched the parallels between abusive religious environments and abuse in intimate partnerships. She has determined that individuals— women in particular—who have been in high-control religious environments are more likely to be in abusive partnerships. These individuals have internalized that their voice doesn't matter, that someone else is allowed to control them, that they are supposed to forgive, and that it would be a sin to leave. The systems are the same whether they are in a marriage, in a church, on a team, or in a workplace. And when our sense of self is eroded or devalued, or when someone who has control over us tells us they represent the will of the creator of the universe, it makes sense that we wouldn't recognize the dynamic happening in another context.

There is something in system theories that we call "first- and second-order change." First-order change is surface change; what we are doing looks different, but the mechanisms driving our current behavior are the same as those driving our previous behavior. Second-order change is transformational and gets to the bottom of what is actually behind our actions. Because people are systems, this applies to us too.

Let's say I am struggling with a shopping addiction; it feels good to shop, but even more than that, it feels painful and anxiety-provoking not to shop. I realize shopping is becoming an issue, so I work hard not to shop. But then I start drinking to help me manage the discomfort. I have changed in one sense but not in another. The thing that the shopping was helping me manage is the same thing that the drinking is helping me manage, which is the anxiety, insecurity, or emptiness I feel inside. Second-order change can come about only when I recognize and address what is behind these coping mechanisms.

When systems teach us to think in a particular way—such as in black-or-white or rigidly controlling or perfectionistic ways—these patterns can become so habitual that doing anything differently feels either scary or wrong. If a system has taught us to mistrust ourselves or that we need to be rescued from the awfulness of ourselves, it's easy to get caught in more systems that teach the same thing. We can easily bounce from one abusive system to the next without understanding why. Or perhaps we do know why but we can't figure out how to do anything differently.

If you are tempted to blame survivors for the abuse they have endured, please resist doing so. If anything, we should step back and marvel at how hard it is to get away, to go on, to heal, when there are so many places and dynamics that reinforce the same patterns of abuse.

Systems as a concept are not bad or good in and of themselves; rather, they highlight the bidirectional nature of influence. The outermost circle moves in one direction toward each individual at the center, but the individuals and smaller communities at the center can also influence the larger circles. While I have introduced systems in a way that highlights how abuse can be proliferated, there is also always the possibility of exerting influence in the opposite direction. Healing forces can move downstream toward us, and our healing journeys can reshape our environment in an outward direction.

Minority Group Stressors and Trauma

As I mentioned previously, academic research is sometimes slow to catch up to what we know in our bones. Religion and spirituality can be helpful for our growth and development, but they can also be harmful. Clinical and academic communities in my discipline are finally catching up to this truth. We now have well-established bodies of literature highlighting the trauma of cults, sexual abuse by clergy, and child abuse by spiritual leaders. In addition, increasing evidence shows that evangelical churches have done particular harm to people who are lesbian, gay, bisexual, transgender, queer, intersex, two spirit, or identify themselves in other self-affirming ways.

In 2022, Joel Hollier, Shane Clifton, and Jennifer Smith-Merry published a paper exploring how queer members of church communities experienced psychological trauma.[5] The authors presented what they call "minority stress theory," a concept linked to the LGBTQI2S+ community through the scholarship of Ilan Meyer.[6] Meyer identified that being a member of a minority group comes with significant stressors that have lasting psychological and physical consequences. Often, these stressors include prejudice, social rejection, feeling the need to hide or conceal parts of their identity, internalized prejudice (in this case, homophobia), or needing coping strategies that help a person blend in. This is thought to be the same for other groups who are marginalized within a dominant culture. This research is essential. It shows that the constant and cumulative stress of discrimination and microaggressions is real, lasting, and damaging.

The researchers interviewed twenty-four individuals from the LGBTQI2S+ community in Australia who had spent at least two years in an evangelical church. They identified the following common causes of trauma in this population:

- Their identity was mischaracterized, or they encountered misinformation or stigma.
- They were told they were a threat to their community and that their community—especially children—needed to be shielded from them.
- Their sexuality was erased in some form because they were not listened to or acknowledged for who they were.

- They experienced relational distancing. They were edged out of their communities in both overt and discreet ways, and those who tried to stay faced leaders' efforts to make them change.

These experiences impacted their social, psychological, and spiritual health in profound ways. Some of them received diagnoses of complex post-traumatic stress disorder, or they were unable to walk past a church without having a bodily activation of the symptoms of trauma. The research validates the impact that members of this community—and many other marginalized communities—have felt but been unable to name. And not surprisingly, the findings also show that in communities where great harm was endured, beautiful, resilient, and powerful solutions to the suffering have emerged. The strength to go on comes at a great cost but is always visible where groups of people have been wounded by those with the most social power. And the evangelical community would do well to learn about what love and faith mean from the people who carry the trauma of rejection by the church.

Going back to ecological systems theory and the five concentric circles, we see there are countless parallels between what happens at the systemic level and what happens at the individual level. It's rare for individual experiences of trauma to happen without there also being widespread systemic problems. In the cases of clergy sexual abuse, such abuse almost always happens in places that ignore, actively hide, or even facilitate the harmful behaviors. We should also acknowledge the failure of systems that leave clergy to suffer on their own, without anywhere to share their private and personal struggles, mental health concerns, unprocessed trauma, repressed sexuality, or addiction. Faith environments that don't allow leaders to be human and seek support outside the church end up with leaders who are more likely to hurt others and themselves.

◆ ◆ ◆

As my patient finished telling me about his dream, tears formed and fell. Mine quickly followed. After feeling trapped for five decades of his life—feeling suffocated by the constriction and control—he was able to look behind the curtain and see the machinery that was behind his suffering. There was a mix of sadness and relief in his tears. Seeing was both painful and liberating. With the grief of knowing how long he had been kept stuck up against the wall, and how close to him the curtain really was, he also felt a renewed sense of aliveness when he realized the on/off button for escape was within his reach.

Seeing the systemic patterns that have kept us stuck, that have hurt us, or that we have used in ways that have hurt others can be overwhelming, but ultimately understanding these patterns can help us see what happened more fully and empower us to make informed choices moving forward.

• PRACTICE •
Orienting Ourselves

After exploring systems, abuse, and patterns inside and around us, we can easily become overwhelmed. Pausing to sense ourselves as bodies can bring our attention back to the system that sits within all the other systems: our mind-body connection in the here and now. This can help us locate the place where we have the most immediate contact with agency so we can begin to repair the mind-body schism that is a by-product of trauma and the systems that create it.

Take a moment to check in with yourself as a body. What are you noticing right now?

Allow yourself to look around. Do this slowly and intentionally. Twist around to look over your shoulder, even if just to look at the wall. Look up to the highest point in your surroundings and down to the lowest point. If you are in a room, see each wall, notice how the light is hitting different objects in the room, and let your gaze rest on something pleasing or neutral. As you do so, allow yourself to really investigate it, perhaps by moving your attention even slower than you were previously.

As your eyes find a place to rest, you might allow yourself to notice what is supporting you in this moment, what is holding you up as a body. Think of the supports under your body (like a chair, floor, bed, etc.) but also consider the ground under the building you are in and the earth always holding you up.

Preston Hill on the Systems and Process of Spiritual Trauma

Here are insights from a conversation I had with Preston Hill about spiritual trauma. Preston is a practical theologian, therapist, and trauma survivor, and his understanding of these ideas brings depth and nuance. You already read some of his rich words above, and here are more on the importance of talking about spiritual trauma beyond the medical model, religious trauma that doesn't arise from an explicitly religious context, and the breakthrough when his clients stop believing they are fundamentally bad.

Preston

Trauma is such a morally saturated experience.

A lot of people don't have the language to recognize that, because people have leaned into the medical model. So we can talk about how the body keeps the score, or trauma as this overwhelming stress response, but there's something still missing: the moral context of trauma, the spiritual dimension, and the spiritual register. This is something that you find universally attested to in trauma studies.

Robert J. Lifton says one of the fundamental aspects of trauma is this profound sense of disconnection. I feel isolated because I experienced something that unearthed my own vulnerability and powerlessness, and I survived and feel ashamed somehow about the way I survived. Something about the way I survived feels gridlocked with shame. And something about this experience has cut me off from the human race.

One of the core components of spiritual flourishing is a sense of connection. I'm connected with others; I'm connected with my world. I feel at home, and there's just a big sense in which trauma cuts me off. I'm no longer at home. There's no longer any home for me, not even with myself. This is a universal experience for survivors of various kinds of trauma. I'd call it almost the spiritual effects of trauma, whether or not the trauma itself was spiritually laden or religiously triggered. This is a universal survivor experience.

This is something that's profoundly moral and spiritual, and it's not unembodied. It's not just stress. It's not just something that can be medicalized. There's something transcendent happening here.

The most parsimonious and operational definition of trauma I found is from an edited volume by Bessel van der Kolk and others: trauma is "an inescapably stressful event that overwhelms people's coping mechanisms."[7] That captures a lot. Trauma is not just the event; it's the post-traumatic symptoms. It's the way in which it lives on in the wounds that remain. It captures the overwhelm; it captures the powerlessness.

I like all of that, but even that definition is kind of medicalized. The way I like to define trauma is it violates your moral expectations, and as a result that violation overwhelms your normal coping strategies and fundamentally alters life afterward.

Another concern of mine is that trauma can become so elastic that it just rips into nothing and doesn't mean anything. Suffering isn't the same as trauma. Trauma isn't suffering; trauma is what is insufferable. That's what's unbearable. Learning to mourn, grieve, and suffer is part of the recovery process to grieve now what you couldn't grieve then.

My colleague Michelle Panchuk says that a better definition of religious trauma could be any traumatic experience that has a religious cause and religious effects. Something about the events that induce the trauma will have triggers that are religious in nature, and the symptoms will be tied with religious images or language. I think about someone who has experienced childhood sexual abuse at the hands of a priest. That is clearly a religious trauma cause. Then the effect would be thinking of someone who's called a father in a community, and then part of my spiritual life is being invited to pray and refer to God as Father, and how confusing and disorienting and outraging that would be. That's not just the overwhelm of a stress response; there's a moral violation happening there.

But there are situations where someone could have spiritual effects from a traumatic experience and the cause was not religious or spiritual. So return to that example: consider someone who's not a religious authority figure, or even a nuclear family authority figure, being the perpetrator of sexual abuse against a child—an uncle or a cousin. Even in that context, lots of survivors will say that the patriarchal language of calling God "Father," even though there's not a one-to-one correspondence in terms of what induced the trauma, there's still a spiritual downstream effect; it doesn't fit. Just as an issue of testimonial justice, we have to have language to account for the spiritual downstream effects of the violence survivors have experienced.

For a lot of my students and clients, the biggest spiritual belief that they have a hard time letting go of is that they are bad. It's kind of learned spiritual helplessness, and they've learned to outsource their spiritual or moral discernment to a spiritual authority. The way that's maintained is through spiritual gaslighting, where anytime they have a moral intuition that is autonomous or involves their own individuation or exploration, which we know is psychologically healthy, they have to code switch. Either they have to remain infantilized psychologically or spiritually to have that kind of congruence, or they have to mature psychologically and come up with a narrative to allow that spiritual infantilizing to remain infantile. To not ever grow up, not ever become autonomous or engage with your own spiritual moral discernment? Gaslighting is a powerful mechanism for that, to believe "I'm bad." I can be psychologically mature, but the greatest sign of my spiritual maturity is that I can't spiritually discern anything on my own. That is so weird and confusing. No one would ever say it out loud, but it's what they live by.

Then some people say, "Hold on, this is weird." There is this nudging process of spiritual exploration, where they eventually realize "That was silly. I'm not spiritually evil. My intuitions for flourishing are good." Then they come to this new level of satisfaction, but a lot of times their prior spiritual and religious communities can't hold that kind of growth. That is a disorientation of its own. They end up becoming spiritually exiled. They have to find new communities.

FOUR

All in the Family

As I write this, my daughter is sixteen months old. She is curious, observant, generous, and playful. She came into the world observing what we do with rapt attention. She has a sweet little stuffed bear that she carries around on her hip. Recently, out of the corner of my eye, I could see the way she smoothed the fur on its head with care and offered it some of her water after she took a drink herself. It all looked so tender, so loving, so familiar.

It was like watching a mirror image unfold right in front of me. This was the same way I offered her water from my cup after I had a sip. The way she smoothed her bear's fur and kissed its nose with her nose was the same way I moved my hand across her head as I breastfed her and kissed her on the nose with my nose when she was done. These were the things we were doing every day, the things that felt normal to us, unconscious even. They were becoming normal to her, shaping her inner and outer world.

Recently, she toddled over to the edge of our bed where my husband was sitting, and he playfully, goofily pressed his face into the comforter and made a "bllululululu" sound. She giggled, and he received a powerful reward and learning neurocircuitry hit—baby giggles, after all, are wildly intoxicating—and he did it a few more times. She started doing it too. As often as possible now, when she sees a bed with a soft, comfy blanket on top, she makes her way over, presses her face into the blanket, wiggles her face around, and makes a funny noise.

After playing with her one afternoon, my mother-in-law told me that my daughter had gone to the edge of the bed in their bedroom and pressed her face into the mattress, wiggling and making silly noises. Without context, my mother-in-law thought this looked and sounded unusual, even while playful and creative. She was not privy to our sacred family ritual that induced fits of giggling in the three of us as we sat pressing our faces into the bed and watching our daughter crack up.

What we as a family do together, even in a silly moment of playfulness, my daughter thinks is how people are together. We laugh about something, and she learns "that's a funny thing to do," and when she leaves our home and goes into the world, she does the same thing, expecting others to laugh with her the same way we do. She may be understandably surprised and confused when she doesn't get the same reaction we give her but will persist nonetheless. These moments highlight the gravitas of parenting: what I teach her will stay with her and will shape her world—not just the little funny moments but what I talk about, how I talk about it, what I believe about myself, what I believe about her, how I talk about her, the way I talk to her. All our interactions influence her inner world, her way of seeing the world, her way of relating to the world. Our interactions are developing her sense of self. Although this can feel a little scary at times, in a healthy way it motivates me to be thoughtful about what I want to teach her.

We were all once developing minds. Of course, we are still developing. We are capable of change, healing, and growth—biologically, we are able to adapt until the moment we die. But we came into the world not knowing that the way we learned how to do things in our family wasn't the *only* way. It wasn't universal to all people everywhere. In our naive, neurobiologically derived infant minds, we can't consider that things could be a different way. What happens around us becomes normal. And all of it shapes the person we become.

We can learn a lot about spiritual trauma by considering our development, our families of origin (the psychological term for the system and culture of the family we were raised in), and what research reveals we need in order to grow in healthy ways. We can also learn what we need to recover that may have been lost and the places we need to go to retrieve the young parts of us that survived things they shouldn't have had to so we can reclaim the fullness of who we are.

Pre-, Peri-, and Post-Traumatic Factors

Whenever I talk to people who have been through trauma, the question inevitably comes up: Why does one person experience something as traumatic and another person doesn't? This question leads us to pre-, peri-, and post-traumatic factors. These are the variables that intersect with the trauma at various points, shaping everything that might make one person respond differently to an event than the person next to them.

Pre-traumatic factors include what a person's life was like before the trauma, their nervous system, meaning-making schema, attachment patterns, strengths, inherited or genetic information and memories, assumptions about the world, and coping and defense mechanisms.

Peri-traumatic factors have to do with how long the trauma lasts, who is involved, if the trauma is relational or accidental, if the person loses consciousness and can't remember what happened or is aware the whole time, if someone is there and doesn't intervene but could have, and so on.

Post-traumatic factors include anything that happens after the trauma: how people respond, if the person is believed, who cares for them, and the systems that are in place that protect the person or reinforce or ignore the trauma.

For example, a person might experience a trauma out in the world and return to a community that surrounds them and believes them. They tell their doctor and are understood. People bring meals and send cards and visit. One friend makes a referral to a trauma specialist; someone else coordinates childcare to ease responsibilities. Another person might experience a trauma out in the world and return home to abusive and distant relationships, no doctor to call on, no memory of what happened, no way to process what did happen, or no idea of where to turn for help.

When talking about religious trauma, if we are lucky enough to have spaces where it is named and talked about, we can do a decent job of identifying the peri-traumatic factors. This is the stuff in the timeline of our lives that we draw a circle around, that has gravitational pull, that demands our attention and haunts our dreams. (We will dive into pre-traumatic factors for religious trauma shortly.) What is tricky about this category is that is implies there is a clear delineation. In some cases of spiritual trauma, an event happens with a clear before, during, and after. For example, a church leader publicly humiliates a person or perpetrates an act of sexualized violence against someone. This we can point at. We can identify when it happened and what it was. But in many cases, there aren't such clear boundaries around a singular event. Rather, trauma resulted from a series of events: it was the cultural water that a person swam in, or it was all the things that happened leading up to the event that eroded a person's sense of self, worth, and voice, making it seemingly impossible in a moment of trauma to do anything except go along with it.

Post-traumatic factors are harder to address when we speak about spiritual trauma, especially in situations where stress builds over time. What happened after the event might include its own traumas, such as the loss of a meaning-making system and community, exclusion or rejection, or fear of eternal torment. This is where, in many cases, the parallel with complex trauma is helpful. Rarely are there single events with a clear before and after.

If you have spiritual trauma, you might be here, living in the post-trauma landscape where the injuries are no longer happening but the memories and imprints of them on your mind and body persist. Or you might be in the middle of it all, trying to figure out why your faith system feels so powerful and painful all at once; it is familiar and meaningful but also connected to anxiety and self-hatred. There is always a time following when the trauma is actively happening. If you are in it, you know that what happens there can add to your healing or add to your hurt. If you aren't there yet, know that it is coming.

In cases where people can identify what happened to them and share their experience with others, there is still such limited cultural understanding of spiritual trauma that people inside the faith community might deny the legitimacy of the traumatic response. In addition, those outside the spiritual community might have no frame of reference for dealing with situations of this sort and may not understand why the trauma is impacting a person so severely. They may not understand how damaging the effects are and could inadvertently shift the blame to the person experiencing it. Even some therapists may not know how to work with religious trauma. Some people seek support from well-meaning clinicians only to feel misunderstood, blamed, or inadequately served. What happens after the trauma, how much we lose, who supports us, who doesn't, how we make meaning of it all, how we process it, or what we do to try to shove it all down—all of this impacts how much our systems experience the trauma as still going on inside us.

When trying to understand why some people experience something as traumatic and others don't, what we talk about the least—but is an essential ingredient—is what happened before the trauma occurred. Again, this is limited in that it implies there was a concrete before and after. In situations of religious and spiritual trauma, there is often a long on-ramp, a series of events that make the moment when something traumatic happened seemingly imperceivable. It can make it hard to do anything about the trauma, can make it feel confusing—such as when the body says "this feels horrible" while the internalized social narrative is saying "this is good church discipline"—may even make the trauma feel good or virtuous for a time.

A significant pre-trauma factor is how old we are when the stressor first happened. When we are an adult, if we have had a secure and safe upbringing and healthy relationships, someone telling us that we are bad might sting or cause confusion, or it might strike us as outright ridiculous. But if someone tells a child the same thing as their world is developing and they lack any other frame of reference, the words shape their development from that point on. In other words, losing a teddy bear at thirty-five feels different from losing a precious teddy bear at five. It is supposed to. Children are vulnerable and deserve to be protected.

In many cases, the pre-traumatic factors of childhood—family narratives, attachment style, and messages about worth, goodness, and self-trust—might be traumas of their own. That means when a person grows up in a spiritual environment where harm is occurring, the pre-traumatic factors that their nervous system got used to all those years ago make it difficult to identify that anything is wrong. This is the upside-down version of the story I told about my daughter nurturing her bear. What we experience growing up almost always feels "normal"; at least, that is the story we tell ourselves unconsciously, even if it is not true. Harmful relationships can include being shamed or punished for asking parents questions; being abused; and being told we are worthless, bad, deserving of punishment, untrustworthy, or fundamentally broken. They can also include neglect or isolation, shame, and highly rigid and high-control parenting styles. If a person emerges from childhood or adolescence or an abusive relationship believing they are fundamentally bad and the cause of their suffering and others' suffering, it's easy to see how seamlessly that would fit into a religious or spiritual context where that idea is supported and a solution is proposed: say a few magic words that make all the bad parts go away.

In other cases, the pre-traumatic factors are social rules that dictate how a faith community functions. These rules may be communicated clearly or in more subtle ways, such as the following:

- Being silenced or punished for asking questions, especially about the practices of the community
- Being expected to share personal information before trust is built

- Being told promises about the future that are used to manipulate
- Subtle shaming of emotions, instinct, or bodily wisdom
- Smearing or lying about those who have left or been critical of the community
- Using welcoming practices ("love bombing") and promises of belonging that are not sustained or become dependent on how well "the rules" are followed
- Suggesting that punishments or consequences are a function of love or protection
- Making a person doubt their experience of reality through denial or outright lying

There is more to this, but you likely get the point: our sense of normal changes. Often, we are led to believe that it is good to question our own sense of truth and rightness, and our connections to people who think differently begins to change.

What We Need from the Beginning

When we get the things we need early in life, it is easier for us to grow up to feel confident, to feel connected to ourselves and others, to give and receive love, to experience our bodies as safe places, to show compassion to ourselves and others, and to have a clear "no" when things are not okay. Think of this as pre-traumatic factors gone right. When we get what we need growing up, we are better equipped to know later in life what isn't okay, what hurts us, and how to get away from it.

In case you have never heard this before, I want to make explicitly clear the kinds of things we need to have, especially in our early years:

- We need to know we are loved and lovable; we must hear it and see it and feel it.
- We need safe, respectful, nurturing touch.
- We need to be protected from violence, whether emotional, spiritual, physical, or sexual. Should violence occur, we need adults to intervene and come to our defense.
- We need to have our cues responded to. If we are angry, sad, hungry, dirty, lonely, or scared, we need it to be seen and validated—even if in that moment nothing can be done to change the circumstances. If we have specific health needs, we deserve medical attention.
- We need to be shown that feelings are important, and we need support to learn how to feel them. We need to know our emotions can be tolerated, that they are not dangerous, and that others won't be alienated by them.
- We need to learn through play, exploration, and making mistakes in ways that are safe and meet our developmental needs.
- We need caregivers who model taking responsibility—including for their own mental health and emotions—instead of blaming others, and who do their best to make a repair when there is disconnection.
- We need to be protected from ideas and experiences that are dangerous or inappropriate for our developmental stage. These include ideas, experiences, and material that are fear-inducing or highly sexualized.

Here is how therapist Adam Young has summarized the basic needs we have early in life (with definitions to follow). We need:

- Attunement
- Responsiveness
- Engagement
- Affect regulation
- A relationship with an adult who is strong enough to handle our emotions
- A willingness to repair[1]

I would add that we need the space and support to explore, play, and learn through mistakes and discovery.

Some of the terms on this list might be new to you. *Attunement* is not just having our needs responded to but having a caregiver who is accurately sensing and perceiving our inner and expressed emotional world and then connecting with us. *Responsiveness* is having a caregiver who is attempting to meet our unique needs. *Engagement* means having present and connected involvement and care without constant surveillance or overprotection. *Affect regulation* is having support with the process of feeling, expressing, and soothing our emotions. This has to happen over years in the context of caring relationships with others for us to be able to internalize these processes and do them ourselves.

Ideally, these needs are met in a fluid and integrated way, where one skill blends into another. For example, attunement often goes alongside responsiveness. Perhaps you are on the phone with a friend and are excitedly telling them something you just saw, but you hear a quiver in their voice, giving you the sense they might have just been crying. As you note their emotion, you shift from an enthusiastic "I am so excited to tell you this" to a slowed-down, quiet "I want to know what is happening. It sounds like you are upset." This is showing both attunement and responsiveness.

If you grew up in a developmental environment that was high in control and fear, you likely did not get the chance to see how vital play, exploration, and mistake-making are to your development. These are the backbones of growing, and not just physical growth and motor coordination but also psychological and relational growth. We need to have the safety to make mistakes, fall down, ask for help, try again, and explore what's around the corner while still being protected from sticking our finger in the light socket, so to speak. Being given the space to get things wrong, to take our time, and to explore requires a caregiver who can tolerate their own discomfort with our risks, who can feel their own impatience without jumping in to take over, and who can tell the difference between a real threat and an inconvenience or preference.

Take a moment to notice what is happening inside you after reading these descriptions. You might feel confused or sad for what you didn't have. Or you might be tempted to minimize these needs. Not surprisingly, if we grew up having our needs minimized, we likely internalized that as a strategy to protect ourselves. As we've discussed, what we experienced as the norm in our childhood shapes the way we are as adults in how we relate to both ourselves and others. So if we are prone to minimize, judge, or ignore emotional or relational needs and their value, there was likely a deficit in this regard during our upbringing.

The good news is that even if we didn't have these experiences, it is not too late to learn how to get now what we didn't get back then. We can still learn how to receive the love, care, and support we deserved so long ago. The research on neuroplasticity shows that there is no such thing as too old, too hurt, or too stuck to change. Our psychosocial selves can adapt, heal, and change right up until the moment we die.

We will talk more about healing in the coming chapters. For now, know that you deserved all these things back then, and you still deserve them today. You likely didn't have these needs met because the existing systems were built by people who likely didn't get their needs met either. Not getting your needs met was not proof in any way that you were bad. And I am sorry if you were ever told that or ever had to believe that to make sense of why you felt so scared or alone.

Why We Return to the Familiar

Whenever I am working with people on meeting the needs that weren't previously met, we often reach a familiar point in our work. I am communicating what is good about them and the things that are true about us as people, and they say, "I believe you, but when it comes to me, it doesn't feel true. Why is it that something that's true doesn't *feel* true?"

You might have asked yourself that question by now. What was normal for us, what we heard or got used to, shapes how we are in the world as adults—including our behaviors, our relationships, and how we feel about ourselves. Said another way, what feels true is often what we are most used to hearing and believing, not what is *actually* true about us. For example, countless lovable, valuable, precious humans are born into families who abuse them, and they often end up feeling unlovable, unworthy, disposable, and alone.

The way we feel about ourselves is akin to the well-worn paths people create when walking through a forest. Taking a path creates an imprint. The more we take the path, and the more the important people in our lives take the path or tell us to take the path, the easier it is to take the path. The terrain becomes worn and familiar. Then we don't even have to think about what we are doing at all; the path seems like the right way to go. And other routes, the untrodden paths with no clear way through, seem arduous, like they are not even a possibility.

Our bodies can get so used to certain experiences or conditions that when we are without them it can feel so disorienting that we unconsciously re-create them. Imagine the person who grew up in a high-conflict home where chaos, violence, and threats were all they knew. Their body is so used to relational unsafety—they've been marinating in it since they were children—that high-stress situations seem normal to them. By contrast, situations of safety and rest seem so unpredictable and unfamiliar that the person experiences those environments and relationships as threatening, scary even. So without knowing it or consciously choosing it, they find ways to create the fear and stress that feel most familiar to their body. Trust and mutual respect seem dangerous, but conflict, as painful as it seems, actually feels more comfortable.

This is called "repetition compulsion." Without consciously knowing it is happening or choosing it willfully, if we have been through something painful, scary, or abusive, especially in a relationship, we gravitate toward the familiarity of that dynamic, thereby repeating negative patterns from our past. Why does this happen? The brain is highly organized around energy conservation and taking shortcuts, so whenever something seems to be programmed in, especially from early in our lives and our close relationships, the energy-budgeting system of our brains can deem changes to our way of thinking, moving, relating, and predicting to be too expensive, too demanding, or outside the budget, so to speak. We can also

get so used to certain levels of stress in our bodies, high relational intensity, or heightened emotional states (including
chaos, fear, and unpredictability) that when we don't experience such things, our bodies can go into a kind of withdrawal.
The things that are healthy or sustainable feel scary or, just as
often, banal and boring.

It seems our brains are wired to feel a sense of normality
with familiar patterns, and we become resistant to change,
even if change is in a healthy and truthful direction. If this is
the case, it is helpful to remember that our wired-in orientation
as humans is both survival and health, even if it doesn't seem
that way on the surface. So when we are in a situation that
reminds us of what we went through before, we can choose to
have it go differently this time—to make ourselves safe in the
present but also to correct course or address the memories of
what happened to us before. This is one way that things can
go. We can do things differently this time around by creating
something new.

In contrast, people can experience a dynamic similar to
what hurt them before, and they feel even more wounded
than they would otherwise. For example, say a child experiences abuse from one parent and goes to the other parent
for help, only to have that parent deny what is happening
and defend the other parent. This leaves the child doubly
betrayed. They are confused by their experience and unpro-
tected from further abuse. Then this person grows up to be
part of a religious community where the leader perpetrates
harm against them. They work up the courage to tell another
leader what happened, and the response is that it couldn't
have happened. They are wrong and are bad for even suggesting it. This feels like the same dynamic they experienced
growing up, adds to the original wound, and makes what is
happening in the present feel even more painful. This is why

experiences in the present can feel hard to recover from or process: the pain has deep roots that reach back into the early years of development.

Even if abuse isn't involved, imagine a child is sad or afraid and goes to their parent to tell them. The parent may respond by denying or ignoring their pain: "You don't need to be sad; nothing is wrong" or "Don't be scared. You're fine. Go on now and make me proud." What if that child grows up and joins a spiritual community that uses the same defense against feelings but with different words. They hear "Don't be sad; God makes you happy" or "Don't be afraid; have more faith." The denial of emotion using a similar strategy of repression and spiritual bypassing, especially when well meaning, can leave a person feeling misunderstood and believing that painful emotions need to go away for them to belong and be okay. (We'll explore spiritual bypassing and its role in trauma in chap. 5.) We know by now that emotions not addressed do not go away. They stay there, lingering, asking to be addressed by getting louder.

Where I start to wince is when faith communities ascribe to God our own defense mechanisms. We discount people's pain and assume God does too, and then we tell people God is on our side as a way of reinforcing our responses and defending our behaviors. We criticize others, judging them for their suffering. We attribute their pain to a lack of faith and say that God does too. We celebrate the people who are most disconnected from emotions and vulnerabilities, those who distance themselves from what feels scary and painful, sexually repressed and controlled. We tell the story that they are the most prized by God or the most faithful. We teach people to hate their humanness and praise them, calling it righteous, because we believe God hates their humanness too. We offer people chronic guilt, shame, and fear of hell and celebrate them as signs of spiritual maturity. We stoke in people an inner critic and tell them it's the voice of God.

I understand that when we hear about the complexity and layers of pain inside us and our bodies we can become overwhelmed, despairing, defensive, or scared. But I want you to know that healing, changing our patterns, and growing in areas that feel "stuck" are totally possible. The beginning of healing may be understanding how we got here in the first place and why it is so hard to do things differently—even if it's good for us. And why things hurt so much—even if we were told it was just a little thing.

The Goodness of Human Development

There are spiritual traumas that can happen to us as adults. Yet what I've learned from working with so many people who have spiritual trauma is that often the trauma is baked into the family of origin or culture or education and is dutifully passed on from one generation to the next and wrapped in spiritual messages. When this happens, the process of growing into a healthy adult is impaired.

There are specific things each of us needs to experience and figure out psychologically to learn how to be in the world. In my field, we call these "developmental tasks." Think of them as lessons or steps in the sequence of growing up that need to happen for us to be fully us in a healthy way. My favorite way to describe this process of human growth and development, especially when it goes well, is that it is the process by which you become more of yourself. You might think of a baby who needs to learn how to stand and take a step before they can run, or how we must learn basic math before we can do our taxes or put together a household budget. In those cases, it makes sense that doing the more complex things later on would be harder, if not impossible, without having the experiences that act as building blocks for what comes next.

In religious families with high control, certain developmentally appropriate tasks and experiences are punished, forbidden, shamed, or called sinful or disobedient. They include developing and expressing one's feelings and opinions, sexual exploration, experimenting with romantic relationships and dating, even lying, boundary pushing, and rule breaking. Each of these is appropriate, even healthy, at certain stages of development. And each is meant to happen at a certain time, when we have people who love and care for us around to help us navigate the complexity, consequences, pain, and joy of how this shapes who we are becoming. Without them, we cannot grow into full maturity, have a secure sense of self, or face the demands and challenges of the world.

Take as an example the toddler who is crying because they aren't getting what they want or are refusing something that needs to happen, like having a bath. The parents can look at this and decide it is rebellious and punish the child. Or they can see that their child is learning to say no because they are figuring out that they have a voice and are testing boundaries. In one sense, the toddler is saying, "Hey, I'm a person, and I have wants and feelings too." They are also implicitly asking, "Will you still love me even if I say no? Even if I have feelings that are different from yours? Will you show me that we can still be close even if we want different things?" and, "Will you help me learn to tolerate the disappointment of not getting what I want?" If their "no" costs them connection, they will probably grow up believing that they have to do what other people want them to do in order to be liked or loved.

Here is an example that is a bit more advanced that might help clarify this. A former mentor of mine, a psychologist who specialized in working with children and teens, told me one time that her daughter lied to her about something. Her daughter hid information from her about the toy she was playing with. This was a toy her daughter was not supposed to be playing with, and so she asked her about it. In a way that was apparently obvious, her daughter lied. My mentor went on to tell me how important this moment was because it presented an opportunity for her to talk to her daughter about lying. They talked about what lying is and when it's appropriate or not to help her explore her internal process about deciding to lie and the consequences for lying, as well as what it means to tell the truth, how and why to tell the truth, and varying layers of honesty and integrity.

Most important, they got to talk about how to feel the feelings that go along with all of this. Mother and daughter both learned important things that day, and the mom got to support her daughter's growth in ways that would have been inhibited if she had gone straight to punishing her. She was able to discern that her daughter was navigating the world, figuring out rules and relationships, and learning about reality, truth, will, independence, consequences, and self-control. The little girl was figuring these things out, but the lie was only one part of the equation. The other part was her experience of how her parent reacted. Together, over time, with such situations happening enough, the two parts will form a story that the girl will carry around inside her about how to be an adult in the world, how to make good choices, and how to relate to others regarding the choices she makes and others make.

Here is what I'm trying to get at: in religious and family environments that are governed by fear and control, some of the normal things that need to happen to help kids grow into healthy selves don't get to happen. The developmental steps—even the basic ones around agency, self-responsibility and life choices, boundaries, rule breaking, and rebellion—are impaired through shame, punishment, fear, control, and re-stricted agency. If development is about becoming more of oneself, and in these environments the self is considered un-trustworthy, sinful, or an obstacle to spiritual maturity, then these environments and the people in them will often do whatever they can to eradicate or impair the development and expression of the self.

As a result, these high-control environments often keep people stuck in a state of psychological and social immaturity. This, of course, can go on for as long as it does because the institution or the parents or the theology portrays the person as good for being like a child, with no differentiated sense of self, no voice of one's own, no desire to think critically. Mean-while, the responsibility for one's life gets placed onto someone else—a parent, a partner, an institution, or a paternalistic God.

Often when people leave families or communities of high control, they have not yet mastered some of the develop-mental tasks their peers mastered long ago, nor have they acquired the appropriate developmental skills. They might try to make up for lost time, realizing there are things they never got to do. In fact, that might be why they leave their faith altogether, even if there are some parts that are good and beautiful about that faith. A new sense of control and agency might lead to a full and empathic "No!" as they finally get to assert their voice. Yet often, being outside the tight reins of moral, psychological, and social control feels like a freefall. They might feel as though they are lost and adrift in their adult lives, with no one to take responsibility for them, no one to show them how to make mistakes and clean up the mess, and realizing that the stakes are a lot higher at age forty-two than at age twelve.

Here is one illustration of how this damage happens. I have worked with many people who were told that if they did not have any sexual contact until they were married, then on their wedding night they would have the most profoundly intimate and satisfying sex possible. But then they realized that their bodies don't, can't, and won't just go from inhibiting something and feeling shame and fear about it to feeling ease, comfort, and confidence about it overnight. That is not how development works. We need to learn skills, and we need places to learn those skills—especially when the skills are relational. A generation of individuals who grew up in the purity movement lack the skills associated with consent, saying no, feeling safe in one's body to explore pleasure and to ask for what feels good, let alone the more nuanced, complex, and satisfying forms of sexual expression that come with knowing one's wants, needs, preferences, and boundaries. I have lost count of how many people have told me that they feel betrayed, deceived, and abandoned by a cultural narrative of purity that promised them intimacy and satisfaction but forbade them from the experiences and education that would have helped them to develop these.

I have also worked with many people who were told as they were growing up in their faith community that their wants were sinful. Their inner sense of truth, clarity, and boundaries was suspect, even dangerous. They come to therapy wondering why, decades after leaving their family home, they can't make decisions for themselves. Whether it's what movie to watch, if they want to commit in a relationship, or where they want to go on vacation, these decisions are out of their reach. Someone described this to me not long ago as feeling like everyone is born with an inner compass, but because theirs was plucked out and destroyed at an early age, they have no internal sense of direction about where to go. While it is true that our ability to feel a sense of "want" and know where it is directed is an extension and expression of the self, in environments where the self needed to disappear in favor of obedience and compliance, the connection to wanting was suppressed.

◆ ◆ ◆

It can be so hard to disentangle all the details of how the hurt happened and how it lives on in us still. We can find ourselves asking questions: What was real? What actually happened? What did I think was good but actually hurt me? What still hurts me but feels stuck inside me? How do I trust myself to sort through all of this when I've been told I'm bad and my heart is deceitful?

It is difficult to do all this sorting, negotiating, and dis-entangling when we have been deprived of the right to self-responsibility, when we feel like we are a child in an adult's body. The next chapters are meant to help us disentangle it all. We'll look at the mechanics of understanding how spiritual trauma happens, how we get stuck in it, and how we can get out. Then from there we will move into healing from spiritual trauma on an individual and systemic level.

I want to leave you with this in the meantime: no matter what happened in your development, whatever occurred in your past that left you feeling stuck will never be more powerful than your inborn human capacity to keep develop-ing. There is a drive wired into us toward growth, movement, and healing. There is a door always slightly ajar with a way out of a stuck pattern or a way of thinking. Even if something in our development got stuck, even if we learned to believe we are unlovable and bad, it is never too late to learn something else. The capacity to change, heal, and grow is alive inside you. And maybe that means you get to do something you never got to do. Maybe that means seeing things in a new way or facing the discomfort of looking at your past and seeing what you never got—or experienced but shouldn't have had to. Even if it's hard for you to believe, know that I hold a relentless and unwavering hope for you and will hold it in my hands until you can hold it yourself.

· PRACTICE ·
Holding and Being Held

As we end this chapter, you might be left thinking about what happened during your development, what you never got, or how you are still developing and how there is time, even right now, to begin to receive the care and tending you have always deserved. Before we ever had words, we had the wired-in capacity to receive touch and care as a way of being supported and soothed. Here is a practice you might try as you tend to yourself now in grief or tenderness, or as you imagine reaching back in time to hold the younger version of you who needed the quality of connection you can offer yourself now.

To get started, find a way of sitting or lying that lets the full weight of your body be held. Shift your position, shape, and direction until you feel like you can let yourself be fully held by what is underneath you. You might try wrapping your arms all the way around yourself, perhaps one around your torso and the other around your neck and the back of your head. Allow yourself to play with posture and pressure until they feel right. If holding yourself does not work or feel comforting, try wrapping yourself tightly in a blanket. After finding a way of resting in which you feel held, take a few breaths and notice what happens. You might stay still, allowing yourself to experience the ways you are supported, or add in some movement—a little rock side to side, front to back, or in a circular motion.

You might imagine that your larger adult self is holding your younger self within your body. Let your younger self know that they now live with you and that you will take good care of them.

Allow yourself to stay in this frame of mind as long as you like, and give yourself some time to transition out of this practice by expanding, stretching, or relaxing out of the holding posture you were in.

Alison Cook and William Matthews
on Learning to See Patterns
That Perpetuate Spiritual Abuse

It is time to meet Alison Cook. I discovered Alison's work when someone forwarded me a very interesting post she made on social media that seemed to effortlessly cut through avoidant spiritual bypassing without erasing the value of spirituality. Since then we have gotten to know each other a little, and I've come to respect her work as a therapist and author deeply. She is the author of three books, including *The Best of You* and *I Shouldn't Feel This Way*, and is a certified Level-2 Internal Family Systems therapist. Her academic work specializes in integrating psychology and spirituality. Her doctoral dissertation is titled "The Role of Reflective Judgment in the Relationship between Religious Orientation and Prejudice."[2] In short, it looks at the role of religious orientation and its impact on prejudice. Yes, I downloaded it. Yes, I read all 193 pages. Yes, it was a Friday night when all of this went down. No, I do not regret my time spent reading her work—it was a highlight of my fall.

Alison

All trauma is probably spiritual trauma on some level. I tend to think about it in really pragmatic terms, along the lines of knowing all trauma causes you to question your worth, to question yourself. Spiritual trauma adds this sort of terrorizing layer that God might question your worth too. That's often subconscious. But as I've worked with people over the years, there is this idea that I know in a sense God loves me or God cares about me, but I don't know it. I don't know it from my body, from my spirit, from my emotions, from my soul.

There are two causes of this wounding that I see. There's what we call more religious trauma, which I separate out a little bit in the connotation of maybe a religious institution. You know, a pastor, someone who's supposed to be the shepherd of a flock causing a trauma, and that's more overt and no less awful. And sometimes it's not overt. There's another way that I have begun to understand spiritual trauma, which is informed by Ana-Maria Rizzuto's book *Birth of the Living God*. She talks about how our parents, our first caregivers, are really our first glimpse of what God is like. God is a very abstract concept as a tiny baby, as a young child. And so even in our homes, even if it's not an overtly faith-based home, there's a way in which we're taught what God is like. And this is terrifying for those of us who are parents. And we do it imperfectly, of course. But there's a way in which we are that first glimpse of what love is, of what kindness is, of what presence is.

And so when for any reason—whether out of neglect, whether the parent has a mental illness, or for whatever unknown reason— that experience of love, of safety, of presence, of comfort isn't there, we pick up a wound. And that wound is a spiritual wound. It's a wound that cuts at those deepest core needs of belonging, of being known, of understanding our purpose—that we matter, that we are valued. And so when we don't get those glimpses of what I believe God represents, ultimately early on, those wounds get created. So all the time I'll see clients who come in, and sometimes this happens in faith settings as well, where a parent will say, "God loves you," and then that parent is absent. You know, they don't show up for you. And so you're like, "Huh, okay. So love means absence." And you go through life and you don't know that's all you know. It's how you perceive love. Or your parents say God loves you unconditionally, but then your parents actually teach you that their love is conditional based on your performance.

Okay, well okay, so God needs me to perform for God. So, these are the more subtle ways where it's not necessarily like you're being taught this awful, awful thing about God that also happens. And I see that too. But there are these more subtle ways that we pick up these spiritual wounds.

That is just what I mean by holy ground when I'm in those moments with people. Because as you know in our work that's like, oh my goodness, now I'm standing in that space with this person. It is a restorative moment. Because when we glimpse that safety in someone else, we start to get a glimpse in our bodies of what God is like, of what love is like.

◆ ◆ ◆

I first met William Matthews III in October 2017. We were sharing the stage at the Liturgists Event in Seattle, and when he was singing I think I literally did a full 180-degree pivot to hear who was making that unforgettably beautiful sound. Not long after we were invited to be cohosts on the podcast together, and he soon became someone I not only love to be around but also look up to. He is equal parts creative genius, incisive cultural commentator, Black history, and *Star Trek* encyclopedia, and he will tell it to you straight, whatever it is, in a way that will hit you square between the eyes. If you're ever able to sit in a room with him and listen to him talk about pretty much anything, you're lucky. I've been trying to peer pressure him into writing a book for years. Maybe taking it to a public level will help. (William, we're waiting on that book, my friend.)

William

What came to mind was this image of trudging through mud: that's what spiritual trauma means for me. It's hard to explain because it doesn't feel tangible like a lot of emotional hurt or abuse. It doesn't feel like you can necessarily grab ahold of it, but it feels just as real. It feels like you're in a fog, and you're just like I can't move this. And I'm trying to see through this or navigate this.

Or that feeling when you walk through a spiderweb, and you can't really see it but it's on you and you feel like you're pulling at nothing. Spiritual trauma is like that. It feels like everything and nothing at the same time, mainly because of how we frame what is an issue, what's not an issue, what's painful, what's not painful, what's real and not real. And so because we can't see our emotions, and because we can't see our insides and what is happening in these chemical reactions, we often think of it as less real, but it's just as real.

Growing up religious felt like I was living in a bunker underground, and every religious experience that I had was one that I believed would hopefully lead me to freedom, that would lead me just a little bit higher. I would get out of one bunker and find a bigger bunker underground and think I was free, ultimately to realize I was just inside another bunker.

I know there's something else up there. I often think kids who grew up religious, we feel like we're growing up at a disadvantage because we're not taught about the world. We're not taught how to take care of ourselves. We're constantly forced to be vulnerable. We're forced to defer to people who don't always have our best interest at heart, especially adults. We're constantly told to lose our power and to give up our power for the sake of this greater reality. And yeah, growing up I was put at a disadvantage by the church, and therefore so much of my life has been about reclaiming power, because I willingly gave it up because I thought that's what God demanded of me.

We take those Scriptures, the Psalms particularly, where David talks about being chosen by God or beloved by God, and we sometimes internalize that to mean our group is special. Theologian Walter Brueggemann talks about this a lot in his work on the Psalms, about Israel saying "I've chosen this," like they thought they were so special that they could get away with anything. They didn't care how they really treated the poor. They didn't care how they treated the prophets or the outcasts or the marginalized. And Israel's sin was always taking this religious zeal and pride to a level that created harm for themselves and others. And when you're in the bunker you feel chosen, you feel special, like "I'm doing the thing that nobody else wants to do. And that makes me better than everyone, makes me better than those surface dwellers, those people in the world out there, or the people who choose to leave the bunker. How dare they leave. Don't they know they're loved by God and we love them." And it's just fear.

I've realized so much of my life was shadowboxing this bogeyman of fear that was really created in my own mind or implanted there in my mind by the spiritual authority in my life. It was this need born out of fear to keep me safe, to keep me hidden, to keep me protected from anything that could have hurt me. And oftentimes it wasn't malicious. I've had to, in my growth and healing, understand that that's not always malicious. Sometimes it is. Sometimes it really is not. I can't think of a day in my life my parents have been malicious toward me. Have they created harm? Have they created situations and belief systems that created harm? Absolutely. And in that way, we can raise those issues, hold people accountable or at least have a dialogue around that. And then there are the people who have created harm, those people in my healing journey I've had to cut out of my life because they were intentional with harm.

We learn that differentiation between who's malicious, who's intentional, who's not intentional. And also there's a spectrum in there of complicity of people being unconscious in their own journey, in their own shadow, and having to hold space for it. Maybe they really don't see. They're creating harm, but they don't see. And when you're in the bunker, it's hard to see. When you grew up in the bunker and you're perpetuating the myth of the bunker, it's hard to believe that there's life aboveground.

FIVE

How We Feel

If you aren't familiar with the world of therapy or haven't taken any helping or counseling skills classes, it might be news that we therapists commonly practice our skills first on ourselves before we bring them into our clinical work. The hope is that in addition to practicing our developing skills, we do the work on ourselves we are asking others to do. I was in a therapist training program a few summers ago where, as part of exploring the childhood wounds we carry into adulthood, we learned about the roles we had to play growing up.

The trainer had us discuss the roles we had to play to defuse the tension in our families and to be who we were expected to be. A role doesn't mean an actual scripted part in a drama per se, but it functions in a similar manner. When we look at dysfunction within family systems, surveying all the family dramas to identify the key parts, we see numerous roles that keep showing up. For example, there is the mascot or joker, who defuses family tension through humor, distraction, or jokes. There is the lost child, who tends to be invisible, forgotten, and silenced (or self-silencing), and the scapegoat, who gets blamed for everything or absorbs the family drama. And there is the hero child or golden child, the one who represents the ideal. These children are very good at doing what is expected of them. They are very perceptive about what makes them valuable and will play that part, even when there is a personal cost. These are just a few of the roles. With each role, no matter how it was portrayed in our family growing up, or how much praise or punishment we got for playing it, there was a benefit to the person and the system in some way. We take on these roles because they have a function—to us, to others, or to the system as a whole.

As this group of therapists was sitting together reflecting on our childhood experiences, the trainer presented the various roles and asked us to raise our hands when he called the role we played in our family growing up. You likely won't be shocked to know that when we got to the role of hero child, almost everyone in the group raised their hand.

People who have dedicated their lives to assisting others, hearing about their pain, and helping them heal were—not surprisingly—carrying the legacy of a childhood in which they learned to give their life away for a cause and be valued for it. This obviously isn't the case for every therapist; I know many therapists who were the black sheep, wanting to talk about the hard truths others didn't want to name, or the lost child, who got really good at listening, observing, and analyzing without expecting to be involved too much in more obvious ways. But those of us together that day all had a good laugh when someone pointed out that we had found a way to make a career out of our coping.

I can think back with tenderness and understanding now to my younger self, who was trying so hard to be a hero. In third grade, I would gather groups of friends who were struggling and give them unsolicited and impromptu life-coaching lessons. I was sure that I had the right answers to help them with their sibling conflicts or could mediate when the esteemed pencil and eraser club had a falling out.

Even as I'm presenting the roles in this way, I am reminded of the complexity of who we are. The thing we learned to do to manage our childhood pain can sometimes shape the most meaningful, rich, and energizing qualities of our adult lives. I think of the child who escapes family conflict into their room to draw, only to become an artist whose work touches so many other people with its depth. Or the child who manages anxiety over their fear of the future by thinking through it logically and then goes on to become a brilliant thinker or theorist. The mystery of being human seems to be that even in our pain there can be beauty and growth: gifts that emerge as evidence of our resilient spirit and capacity to adapt. Yet sometimes the strategies that helped us survive cut us off from the fullness of who we are or could be.

If spiritually traumatic systems claim the label "family" to broker unearned trust, then it may be wise for us to take that label at face value and analyze these communities using family systems theories. We should begin to see them as the dysfunctional family systems they are, whereby the survivors bear the legacies of the roles they had to play to survive these systems and keep the peace. Some are banished into the role of scapegoat so others can have a place to point the finger. They are often those who challenge the system, tell the truth, or disavow the rigid and authoritarian expectations. Others are banished to the role of lost child—silenced and pushed aside—never given access to the inner circles of power. And most often, the hero child is groomed from childhood to have the pressure of eternity placed on their shoulders. The souls of others become their responsibility, engendering and venerating a compulsive drive to rescue.

The Drama Triangle

The word *rescuer* might conjure different images for each of us: the first responder on the side of the road pulling somebody from a car wreck, the community member fostering homeless dogs, or the lifeguard at the beach helping someone caught in a riptide. We might think of the things we do to rescue or what kinds of situations put us in need of rescue.

I want to invite us to step back and think more analytically and systematically about the rescuer role. Let's consider its undercurrent of motivating factors. Of course, helping others is good and important, but in spiritually abusive systems selfless caring on behalf of others is both insidiously taken advantage of and rewarded—and there are cumulative costs for the person doing all that rescuing.

When the word *rescuer* comes up in this way, I think of Karpman's Drama Triangle. This is a social theory developed in the 1960s that provides a map for destructive patterns of power and conflict in relationships, by (often unconsciously) relegating one person to the role of victim, another to persecutor, and the last one to rescuer.[1] Triangles, when they are used to explain systems of people, can be traced back to the work of Murray Bowen, a psychiatrist who pioneered the development of a family therapy.[2] Bowen saw that dynamics between two people can easily cause tension, so a third party is engaged to reduce the tension. While forming a triangle keeps people from actually addressing and changing the conflict, it can create a sense of stability. The tension gets shifted around instead of worked through, and with three people instead of two, there are more places for the tension to be held and dispersed. If this sounds complicated, just bring to mind a time when you were irritated or hurt by someone, and you found it easier to tell a friend all about how awful the other person was rather than going directly to the person to let them know that what happened was not okay. Venting to an uninvolved person about how wronged you were can feel relieving, especially if you grew up with a fear of conflict that causes you to avoid direct confrontation.

In Karpman's Drama Triangle, the victim is not necessarily an actual victim but rather a person who acts or feels like they are one. They are usually convinced they are powerless and that any efforts to change are futile. As with everything we do, there is a purpose or a payoff to this. Being the victim allows us not to have to face change, take responsibility, or make choices. Those in the victim role love to have a rescuer save them and a persecutor as someone to blame for feeling stuck.

The rescuer, on the other hand, enables the person to stay a victim. The draw of being able to save helps them feel powerful, good, and useful. But given how committed the victim is to staying a victim, the rescuer can't necessarily get what they need by being able to rescue, which is both a way to feel good and a way to avoid their own pain. They often feel guilty if they don't rescue, and they can become the persecutor if the victim doesn't change.

The persecutor is sometimes also called the villain. This is the person who likes to blame and say, "It's all your fault." They are often controlling and rigid and take a position of superiority. But when they are confronted about this pattern, they may lash out or start to identify as the victim. The persecutor likely doesn't know how to ask for their needs to be met in a vulnerable and relational way, one that does not use power or control.

This might sound familiar. You likely saw a drama triangle in your family at one point or another. You might find yourself in one right now or remember a time you were caught in a triangle. Perhaps you found yourself hurt by a choice one parent made, so you went to the other to complain. Or you may have seen one in a work setting: coworker A is always trying to help coworker B solve problems with coworker C. Sometimes it's easier to tell someone else we are hurt than the person who hurt us. For many of us, this is what we learned in our first family, our family of origin. Our family of origin is our first experience of being in a group, where we come to understand and experience the pull of implicit group rules about behavior and belonging. It is also the place we learn so many of the skills we have for navigating conflict—or not—and acquire the voices we carry around inside our heads. We often learn how to talk to ourselves by picking up how the people who cared for us talked about us and how they talked about themselves.

You might be wondering why I'm talking about a family systems triangle in a book about spiritual trauma. The idea hit me a few months before I started working on this book, when I was trying to explain to someone what is particularly insidious about spiritual trauma in religious environments. In spiritual environments of high control, a person is often told they are bad to their core. An evil lives inside them, and they are powerless to stop it from taking over and ruining their life and causing eternal suffering, unless—get ready for it—they are rescued by someone outside themselves: a system, a doctrine, a right way of believing. All three roles are represented: the victim, the persecutor, and the rescuer. When we are in these spiritually abusive contexts, there is still a triangle created, but *people are told that both the victim and the persecutor live within them.* That leaves a person trapped, at war inside themselves; the only way out of the conflict, to quell the storm inside, is to have someone swoop in to rescue them.

I don't want to diminish the suffering involved in believing you are both evil at your core and powerless to do anything about it. It creates a distress and inner conflict that can torment a person their entire life. It understandably creates a powerful gravitational pull toward any person, system, story, or belief that promises to alleviate the internal tension or transcend it all together. It doesn't help that the system or person who promises to help in this toxic dynamic is usually also reinforcing the idea of the continual badness of people. Said another way, this is like a doctor providing a medicine that both causes and treats a wound at the same time. The cure is also the cause of the harm.

The other connection to religious and spiritual trauma is how important it becomes to be a rescuer if other people are victims and the persecutor is culture, or Satan, or their own humanity. If the persecutor brings not only distress and suffering but also torment that lasts for eternity, becoming a rescuer is compelling. But more than that, it becomes essential both for saving your own soul and for demonstrating how much you care for others—as evidenced by a commitment to trying to save others' souls. In other words, this is the savior complex. The rescuer does the rescuing as a means of relieving their own pain or anxiety, shirking self-responsibility, and turning outward instead of looking inward. The rescuer needs a victim to sustain this. I can't think of a better solution to the perpetual need to play the rescuer than to imagine that every person in the world is a victim.

Wired into Us from Birth

While we're on the topic of triangles, I want to introduce another triangle that helps make sense of the trauma that happens to us and within us in certain spiritual contexts. This is called "the triangle of experience" and comes out of my training in a kind of therapy called Accelerated Experiential

Dynamic Psychotherapy (AEDP).[3] The triangle of experience provides a map for our inner worlds and helps explain why people are stuck and experience so much distress or struggle to feel calm, confident, connected, and compassionate (see fig. 5.1).

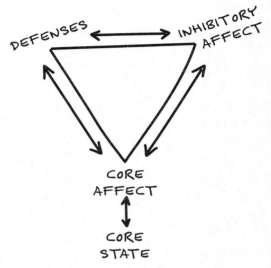

Figure 5.1. Triangle of Experience

Here's how this triangle connects to spiritual trauma. Emotions are core to who we are as people; they are wired into our species and represent our personhood and identity. We are born with the instinct to feel feelings and express them. Think of a little baby, who doesn't have words to talk about being angry or sad or excited or scared, only shaking limbs, smiles, laughs, and tears. Analysis about core emotions (or what we call "affect" in the clinical world) varies ever so slightly from researcher to researcher, but the main unifying theories suggest that our bodies get into certain states that are important for our social and physical survival. These states have action-directed impulses wired into them, and these impulses are *somatosensory*, which means they are bodily before they are ever words or thoughts.

When we name these physiological states of charge that we are born with, we call them fear, anger, sadness, disgust, joy, excitement, and desire (or sexual excitement). These feelings are written into our bodies and help us solve problems and communicate what is important to those around us. Remember, our nervous systems evolved a long time ago. Sometimes our impulses don't make sense when we're sitting in a coffee shop drinking a latte and reading a book, but they do make sense when we remember that our bodies developed these responses in more primitive conditions. Our ability to signal to other members of our family or tribe that a berry is poisonous or there is a threat on the horizon could mean the difference between life and death. Each core affect has a purpose: fear gets us away from danger; anger protects what we value and clarifies boundaries; sadness communicates loss and the need for comfort; excitement helps us celebrate and motivates us toward what is pleasurable; and desire directs us to experience expansion, satisfaction, and self-expression.

You might already be having a reaction to this information. You wouldn't be alone if that is the case. Desire born into us? No! Anger is good and part of protecting what we love? No way! And how can being afraid ever be a good thing? It means you don't have trust, right? I'd like to explain why you're having a reaction and where that comes from. Your only job right now is to notice your reaction and stay with me a little longer.

Remember what I said about emotion being wired into us from birth and signaling to those around us what we need? A baby can't say, "Mom, I'm hungry. I need a bit of milk. You must be stressed and forgetting I'm hungry, so I just wanted to politely remind you." That has never happened, nor could it. A baby cries to get the caregiver's attention; that is all they have.

The adult holding the hand of a child stepping into the street has fear show up in their body when they see a car coming. The fear comes with a shot of adrenaline that activates their leg muscles, makes their heart pump faster, and causes their pupils to widen. This bodily reaction helps the adult quickly jump back off the street onto the curb and pull the child with them. The child sees the face of their normally calm parent change and knows there is danger; they get scared too, but it helps them act fast and stay close to the caregiver. Emotions are as much physiological as they are social. So when we grow up and have feelings, they are meant to be seen and supported by those around us.

Here's the problem: not everyone around us loves our feelings. Family, culture, community, religion, peers, educational environments, and the key people around us communicate to us the rules of belonging. They might see our anger and shame us with anger of their own. We might have fear and be told to shove it down. Sadness, pleasure, and excitement can provoke a negative response from the key people in our lives. We are told they are bad, can't be trusted, and are dangerous. Or more often, we aren't told directly but learn through our experiences that when we feel anger, we will be dismissed or disciplined; when we are sad, we will be seen as being ungrateful; when we feel excitement, we will be given embarrassed looks and scolded about pride. And we learn that desire is never, ever mentioned. The communication about emotions can be covert or overt, but we learn that to keep the peace, to be "good," to stay in connection (which as a child is as important a need as shelter and food), to be safe and avoid harm or abandonment, feelings have to go away or be pushed down.

Why does this happen? We store inside our bodies the maps of what we learned early on. Feel scared? Get shamed. Then, in relationships with others, we act in the ways that were modeled for us. This isn't the kind of memory we can articulate or narrate; it's the kind of memory that is stored in our bodies. We call it "procedural memory." It is the kind of memory that allows us to ride a bike or drive a car without having to think through the steps each time. If you think back to your childhood, you should consider that what your parents did to you in your feeling states was likely done to them by their caregivers when they were kids and showed those same emotions.

There can be a million reasons why our parents have trouble tolerating our feelings: life events, our parents' parents, culture, race, gender socialization, age, and so much more. But one of the factors most related to this conversation is our religious and spiritual contexts. Some parents have actually been told by faith leaders—who are somehow regarded as child development and psychology experts—that kids' emotions are bad and need to be shamed, hit, or neglected out of them. This includes paddling and the famous "paddle with holes" phenomenon that, let me be very clear, is child abuse, even if covered in Christian wrapping. Some of the religious values we or our parents were raised with communicated that feelings were untrustworthy and even sinful. Fear was proof we didn't trust God. Anger was the mark of a wicked heart. Sadness was proof we didn't have the joy of the Lord or did not appreciate all we had been given. Excitement was okay when it was about something God was doing but not about our own accomplishments or who we are. Desire? Unless it's for the Lord, forget it. Want nothing except what you are told to want. So what did we do? Our developing systems adapted to the world around us; we learned quickly what was not okay or got us punished or made us feel unlovable.

As we develop, our nervous systems will always choose connection over autonomous self-expression. So even though our emotions are wired into our bodies—in the same way digestion, blinking, and fatigue late at night are—the way we stay in relationships is to move up the triangle of experience. At the bottom of the triangle is the affect. The top right and left corners of the triangle represent something else: inhibitory affect and defenses.

Inhibitory affect is shame, guilt, and anxiety. They show up in our bodies the same way other feelings do. But unlike other emotions, they are learned. They signal that we are getting close to something we shouldn't be getting close to. They warn us by making us feel horrible, so we back away. For example, if I was told growing up that anger is a dangerous thing for a Christian woman to feel, then I would learn to do anything I could to get away from anger. And anytime anger squeaked through the door, I might feel guilt ("Oh, I did a bad thing by getting angry") or shame ("I'm a sinful human for feeling anger") or anxiety ("What will happen to me now that I got angry? Will God punish me?"). These aren't feelings that communicate about our needs and help us find solutions; rather, they are feelings related to learned responses—usually something we learned to feel in relationship to something else.

I commonly hear people in therapy talk about the role of shame as inhibiting desire. A person hears that desire is wicked, then feels desire or expresses it some way and is told it is sinful or dirty. When this happens enough times, a person internalizes the shame to the point that even if no one else is around telling them that what they are thinking, feeling, or doing is bad, an inner monologue shames them, and they believe it is the Spirit convicting them.

The existential and spiritual pain of shame, the consuming nature of anxiety, and the sickening feeling of guilt are often so intolerable that we move over to the other corner of the triangle of experience to manage them. There lie our defenses.

Defenses are anything we do to get away from feeling our core emotions, being in contact with our inner world, or escaping from inhibitory effect: scrolling on our phones, using a mind-altering substance, masturbating, eating, not eating, playing video games, denying, dissociating, isolating ourselves, talking nonstop, joking, intellectualizing things, being violent or aggressive, controlling, helping other people, or using spiritual practices. Here, you might notice some discrepancies: How can you say that sexual desire is good and a core affect and masturbation is a defense? How can eating and not eating both be defenses? And if spirituality is a core feature of our humanness, how can spiritual practices be defenses?

How something is used is what makes it a defense. The things we do become defenses when we do them to get away from our inner emotional experiences. The kicker here is that this doesn't always happen consciously. If we have been doing something to distance ourselves from our feelings for a long time, we can get so skillful at it, so polished, that we don't even know it's happening. The people around us may notice it more than we do. But that gets harder when they too are defensive in the same way.

The Defense of Spiritual Bypassing

One significant defense in religious contexts is *spiritual bypassing*. The term was coined by John Welwood to identify the use of spiritual practices and ideas as a defense.[4] It means we sidestep, skirt around, or avoid underlying emotional issues or problems in our lives or in the systems we are a part of by using prayers, mantras, and promises that are positive—like compulsive rituals that keep us from feeling anxiety or fear. This can look like believing we are spiritually superior for not succumbing to our emotions. It shows up when we minimize suffering or celebrate it as part of God's plan. When we re-spond with platitudes, we reject the experiences of others that force us to face pain—theirs, ours, and others'. This happens in spiritual contexts where nonattachment and self-denial are seen as signs of spiritual maturity. No bad vibes are wanted here, only positivity. We wrap up our painful experiences, unanswered questions, and trauma in a spiritual package and give it nice language, which has the added benefit of making it more attractive and garnering moral value in the eyes of others. I believe this happens more than we know. It is so au-tomatic, so venerated in some communities that it's not only not recognized as avoidance but also considered the very best, most ideal way to be.

Spiritual bypassing is very hard to overcome in a thera-peutic setting. As a form of avoidance, it is so valued and reinforced that it can be quite challenging for a person to ac-knowledge it. Not spiritually bypassing can feel terrifying, re-associating the person with the anxiety, shame, and guilt they feel and taking away their coping strategy. It can be downright befuddling for a person who has been praised for being skill-ful at spiritual bypassing to realize there might be something harmful about praying away their fear—or whatever defensive practice is in view. The goal of the triangle is ultimately to help us connect better with what is actually happening inside us. Acknowledging our inner experience allows us to sit with it, to feel emotions and allow them to move through us.

Processing emotions might seem confusing at first if you never learned how to do this growing up or were told your emotions are harmful. But avoiding and suppressing emo-tions are what harms us, not the emotions themselves. When we learn how to feel and allow the feelings to move through our bodies in the way they naturally want to, they actually pass. They come like waves rolling in and building until they crest and then settle on the other side. Experiencing them allows them to move through, not suppression, shaming, control, or avoidance. If only faith-based parenting groups understood affective neuroscience. I like to dream that this would mean that instead of perpetuating strategies of abuse, control, domination, and shame, parents would learn to feel their *own* feelings as a mark of the goodness of their bodies and then pass that ability on to their children and their communities. Instead of resorting to spiritual bypassing, we need to change the systems that did not allow us to express our emotions.

Ultimately, the triangle of experience allows us to track where we are in our inner process. It teaches us to ask: Am I using a defense? Am I experiencing an inhibitory affect? Am I feeling a core emotion? The triangle helps us learn to listen to our emotions and feel them as sensations so they can move through us. On the other side of this process is something called "core state." It is our wired-in default setting as humans: it is calm, clear, connected, compassionate, courageous, creative, coherent, and collaborative. It is where our systems are wired to live when we are not feeling an emotion that signals something important is happening.

This might be revolutionary to hear when we have been told over and over that we are wired as bad from the start. It might grate against a deeply lodged belief that we are utterly unacceptable and unlovable. I am here to tell you that from a scientific, psychological, and research-informed perspective, this is not the case. You were born good; we are all born good. We never questioned that or thought otherwise until some other message was hammered into us. It is possible to pick up the story of our badness accidentally, especially if we come from situations where no one ever intended us to believe that. But I believe it is a form of spiritual and psychological abuse to be told that our fundamental nature, the core of who we are, is bad.

If that feels familiar or if it happened to you, I am so sorry. I wish I had a time machine so I could go back to those moments, grab the microphone, look you square in the eyes, and tell you that you are good—exactly as you are, exactly as you came into the world. It is your true nature to be connected, to feel pain and joy with others, to want to help, to ask for help when you need it, to be able to rest and receive love, to want good for others, to have hope for the future, and to have love in your heart and wonder in your eyes. That has always been true of you, and I know that, because it's true of each of us. Being told otherwise should never have happened.

I find the triangle of experience helpful when thinking about spiritual trauma for the following reasons:

- As mentioned above, you might have been told that the thing under the feeling is your badness. That's a pretty big deal. It can change our lives, our relationships, our view of the past, and our view of others to believe otherwise.

- You might have learned that an inhibitory affect is the conviction of the Spirit or proof of spiritual maturity instead of a socially acquired braking mechanism that signals what you had to avoid to maintain belonging. It can also be used as proof that you don't know what is true about you; the suggestion is that you have anxiety because you don't believe God holds your future. That's confusing.

- Defenses are confusing too because they are somehow both proof of our badness (your mental health issue is a sign you don't have faith, your substance use means you don't trust God, etc.) and proof of our value (pray away your fear, give all your time and money to this community, have an airtight, black-and-white theology so you don't have to fear what happens after you die, and so on).

Learning to Feel Again

There are two helpful takeaways when it comes to the triangle of experience. First, it can be so relieving to know the information. Our shame can decrease, and we might feel a spark of insight or recognition knowing there is a tool for making sense of our internal distress. Second, it helps us see a way forward. We can know what we might do next to help us reconnect with our core self.

When we use the triangle, we might start by mapping out where we are on it in the moment. Are we experiencing an inhibitory affect? If that is the case, we can ask, What feeling or feelings might be underneath it? What might we be trying to avoid feeling? Sometimes our feelings are about the right now, and other times they are waiting for our attention because there was never room to feel them in the past. If we can manage to get underneath our defenses or the strategies that keep us away from our feelings, then we might be able to identify them—noticing the sensation in our bodies and the intensity of a rising emotion. Then we can slow down and ask, What is the feeling I feel in all of this?

Sometimes our feelings show up first as the words we give them. Especially if we find it hard to pay attention to and trust our bodies, we might notice the word *sad* or *angry* or *scared* or *happy* resonates with us, but it's hard to feel the sensations of the emotion. Emotions are energy that rises and moves and communicates through our bodies, but when we have learned to mistrust our bodies and the signals they send, it makes sense it would be hard for us to feel or to know what to do with that feeling.

To get back to our core state, we have to stay with the feelings. The first step might be learning that our feelings are not dangerous but rather provide important information that needs our attention. They show up in our bodies and can be trusted when we build relationships with them and learn how to process them. Each emotion, like many things in nature, comes in wave form. As we feel the intensity of an emotion build, our old instinct to suppress it comes up, but if we can stay with it as a series of sensations, it will peak and come down on the other side of that wave. On the other side will be some instinct, insight, or direction on how to act and where to go next.

If feeling feelings is new for you, it can be scary. You might want to diminish the process or reject it, especially if you were shamed, belittled, rejected, devalued, punished, or left alone when you felt feelings before. Those responses from others, especially from important people in your life, are often lodged inside your nervous system. The responses are still there to keep you in line with other people's expectations or values so you can avoid being wounded in some way. If you notice you are suppressing a feeling, you can try saying to that part of yourself that is attempting to suppress it, "I am so grateful for you and how you helped me belong and survive in my environment. I'm here now, and I would like to feel this feeling just a bit more than I did before. If it gets to be too much, we can stop."

Here are some of my favorite strategies for staying with a feeling as it rises. Of course, all of this depends on knowing you're feeling something. If feelings in a general sense are new to you, you might search online for an image of a feeling wheel and look at the different emotions. Sometimes having them listed and grouped in front of you can help you determine what might be stirring inside.

Once you have a sense that an emotion is present, do the following:

- Remember the emotion is not dangerous and say to yourself, *I can feel this and survive.*
- Determine where the emotion is in your body. What does the sensation feel like? Does it feel like tightness or expansion, cold or hot, or both at the same time in different places? What does it want to do, how does it move, where is it going?
- As you notice the sensation, try to keep your attention on it. Imagine you are breathing right into the epicenter of the feeling and allowing the breath to surround the sensation. You can also imagine watching the sensation with your mind's eye. I like to call this bird-watching. When we bird-watch, there is no agenda, no need to fix or change the birds, nothing but watching what the birds do next, keeping track of their motions, and trusting they will come and go as they please. When we bird-watch, we simply pay attention to the sensation and see what happens next.
- You might notice a word comes to mind, or an image or a thought or a desire for action. Keep track of it, and return to the felt sense in your body.
- If you know you are feeling something and are afraid to go into it, you might bring in a person to be with you as you move forward—someone you trust who will listen and make space for your feelings and will help if you get stuck. If no one is around, you can do this with your imagination.

- While you might have the urge to run with a feeling—to let your fear pick you up and carry you far away, or your anger make you want to yell out loud and hit something—what is healthier and more necessary is being with the sensation. Underneath the desire to run away might be a jittery sensation running down your legs. The anger might come with a burning heat or a wave of tightness in your arms. Noticing the sensation won't hurt you or anyone else; it is not dangerous. If you sense that your anger wants to move you to react, you can clench your fingers or jaw or take some deep breaths. If you experience fear, you can jump up and down, clench your leg muscles, or move them really fast on the spot.

Feelings are created not for violence but rather for protection, expression, and flourishing of self and community. When you can slow down and stay with a feeling, you will see what is so good about it.

As difficult or uncomfortable as they are, feelings can last only so long. The intensity is not meant to exist indefinitely; our bodies wisely know how to move us through them and discharge the energy—as long as our defenses don't get in the way. On the other side, we feel ourselves slow down, settle, take deeper breaths, relax our muscles, and get a sense of what happens next.

Doing this over and over with little feelings helps us build trust in our bodies and our capacity to stay with feelings as they rise and fall. Learning that I can sense the little contraction of nervousness in my belly or the slight drop of my shoulders in disappointment helps me know that in the future I can venture into the bigness of my biggest fear or into the depth of my deepest sadness. How we respond to our feelings helps us build trust with ourselves.

Returning to Ourselves

A hallmark of psychological maturation and health is when we make space in our adult lives to look back on where we have come from, what shaped us, and the gifts and wounds we carry as a result. Doing this allows us to see that we came into the world whole, and it was only in our unconscious strategies to adapt and connect, survive and belong, that we had to stifle parts of ourselves, leaving us with rigid roles to play and little flexibility around them. The process of remembering helps us to move forward—more embodied, more connected, and with a better sense of our whole self.

While spiritual trauma happens in obvious places like churches, synagogues, temples, mosques, and ashrams, there is also spiritual trauma, or the possibility of it, anywhere there are groups of people. Such trauma happens when there is a devaluing of others, when leaders manipulate and control and trick people into following them, and when institutions cover up their mistakes by discrediting accusers or pretending that damaging behaviors never happened. There are also less obvious forms of spiritual trauma, such as people telling children they were born bad or communities ostracizing, problematizing, and shunning people for their disabilities— telling them they are broken and in need of healing prayer. And then there is the wholesale stealing of Indigenous land, and the building of a nation on it based on the churches' Doctrine of Discovery, and the subsequent wiping of this reality from the dominant culture's history books in favor of a story that obscures the truth. I believe it is possible to experience spiritual trauma—and either benefit from it or perpetuate it— without ever knowing it's happening.

While considering this can tempt us to fall back into our bypassing ways, I urge you to consider the words of one of the prophets of our time. Audre Lorde wrote, "The master's tools will never dismantle the master's house."[5] In other words, it will take something different from the tools we were handed by toxic and abusive systems to build communities where spiritual trauma doesn't happen. We do something different each time we refuse to believe we are bad. With the courage of an open heart, we can stay connected to the pain within ourselves, we can see the pain we have caused in others, and we can hang on to the ray of hope that comes from telling the truth about what should not have been and who we really are.

◆ ◆ ◆

I want to end this chapter with one of my favorite poems. I read it often when I speak about emotion and healing our relationships to ourselves. It was written by the thirteenth-century Persian poet Rumi and translated into English by Coleman Barks.

The Guest House

This being human is a guest house.
Every morning a new arrival.

A joy, a depression, a meanness,
some momentary awareness comes
As an unexpected visitor.

Welcome and entertain them all!
Even if they're a crowd of sorrows,
who violently sweep your house
empty of its furniture,
still treat each guest honorably.
He may be clearing you out
for some new delight.

The dark thought, the shame, the malice,
meet them at the door laughing,
and invite them in.

Be grateful for whoever comes,
Because each has been sent
As a guide from beyond.

· PRACTICE ·
Emotional Awareness and Self-Care

After reading a chapter like this, it is appropriate to stop and ask ourselves about feelings. This is useful both because of the reactions you might have to what you read and as a way of practicing skills that might still be relatively new to you. I like to try this practice at regular intervals through the day, or in moments when I sense something in my body that signals I need to slow down and tune in.

Start by stopping whatever you are doing and finding a supporting and settling posture. You might want to close your eyes or let them rest by focusing forward. Try to notice what emotions you are feeling right now. If you can think of an emotion word, try asking yourself what sensations you experience that coordinate with that word. Try noticing things like temperature, moving energy, pressure, space, or other qualities.

If you are struggling to notice an emotion, try to think of an emotion that would obviously contrast with what you feel right now. You might remember a time you felt that emotion. How is that different from what you are experiencing right now? You could also take time with each of the core emotions (fear, anger, sadness, excitement, desire), remembering a time when you felt each of them.

As an emotion emerges and you track it in your body, see if you are able to breathe into it, staying with it a little longer than you typically do. Perhaps you can bring to mind someone you love, trust, or feel close to (even if you don't know them personally), and imagine them sitting next to you as you feel this feeling. Let them reassure you that you are good and lovable even as you feel this feeling.

Laura Anderson on Power, Control, and the Savior Complex

Laura Anderson and I had an illuminating conversation about spiritual trauma and its effects. If you are new to her work, please find her book, *When Religion Hurts You*. Laura holds a master's degree in marriage and family therapy and a PhD in mind-body medicine. She is the founder of the Center for Trauma Resolution and Recovery, an organization that focuses on working with folks who have experienced high-demand, high-control religions or cults, and in 2019 she cofounded the Religious Trauma Institute. That is the long and impressive way of saying that Laura is the perfect person to hear from about the saving and rescuing dynamic in the context of spiritual trauma.

Laura —————————————————————————————

When I was going through my own deconstruction process, a pivotal moment came a few months after I had ended a domestically abusive relationship. I was going through my journals and trying to piece together *How did this all happen?* I felt very confused because I couldn't tell if my abusive ex-partner had said certain things or if that was God and the leaders in the church.

At the time I was specializing in domestically violent relationships and had a lot of resources at my fingertips. So I started digging in and noticing all these correlations between what we might consider a spiritually abusive environment, or a system that is built on dynamics of power and control, and the dynamics of power and control in domestically abusive relationships.

As we're talking about the role of the hero, the rescuer, in religious contexts, we're looking at this being a first invitation. God loves you so much. Jesus died on the cross for you. At least in evangelical Christianity, there's a savior figure. You are this person who's worthless, who should not even be allowed to take a breath. You are ground down into this worthless thing. But then there's this savior who's there to pick you up and to literally and figuratively give you life. We see this in abusive relationships as well, where there's this flooding of all these things that someone— the rescuer, the abuser—can do and be for you. But in a religious context, it's the savior figure who's coming to save you from yourself and give you the life that you've always dreamed of. And that can initially get people into a system where they're now saved, where they are now able to experience life in a whole new way.

But just like abusive relationships start to move into a period of tension, to become a little bit more tense in this push-pull, if you really were committed to this savior figure, then you would want to share that with everybody else. And it really can become, rather than a gift, a responsibility to share with other people. And if I don't, that calls into question if I'm actually committed to my savior. We frame it as a gift. Because that sounds really good, but in reality it's coming from our place of obligation to rescue you. And so it also then becomes this very heavy burden that we carry.

When we hear these messages and participate in these experiences over and over, they become embodied, even if we were to leave an environment like that. And we tend to play them out in a different way, whether that's in relationships, family contexts, peer-to-peer relationships, advocacy work, social justice, all sorts of different ways where we are proselytizing for a different message. But those same dynamics are at work within us.

When we are taking on that identity of the hero, the rescuer, "I must save you," it's not necessarily aligned with our authentic self, because we've tended to take on the identity that the system, the family, or the relationship has assigned to us. So to be a true believer, here is what you say and do, here's how you relate, how you dress, here are the things you laugh at and the things you don't laugh at. A pastor of mine told me a long time ago that truth and life are prescriptive. Everything was prescribed for us. So there wasn't really that much room to show up as an individual, if it did not match the prescribed way of living. And I'm now supposed to save others. We are saving them to this idea of who we are supposed to be, what life is supposed to be, rather than offering them the ability to show up and live freely as themselves.

When we bring out this prescriptive identity, and we say here's essentially the right way to be and to live, to exist in this space, that means that anybody who does not subscribe to what that is essentially becomes dangerous. In our nervous systems, difference often equals danger. And this can give us reason to distance ourselves from them. And maybe that's kind of the most generous way we can exist. But in other cases, it can give permission to harm other people, whether through overt physical harm, hateful language or speech, or creating narratives that ostracize and oppress.

And that leads to all sorts of divisions, whether within familial settings or cities or workplaces, all the way to our countries. I can look at different dynamics within the United States and other countries as well, where if you don't believe certain things, you are considered to be dangerous or harmful.

I still vividly remember the day I was standing in my kitchen and realized that mission trips were colonization trips. It was a very humbling moment. I can have so much empathy for my younger self or the groups I was a part of, because I really did believe I was doing a good thing. And yet, as I learned and grew, I was also able to say, "Oh wow, yeah, that was really, really harmful." In this case, in so many cases, it really is White saviorism saying, "We have the answers for you. We're going to come into your culture, into your space, and tell you that what you are doing is wrong because it's not the way that we are doing it." There's this savior piece of it, because we have a savior for you. It's the savior we've created.

I can empathize with people who haven't done work around this and believe that they're doing the right thing [on trips like this]. Research even tells us doing this is not helpful. In fact, it is quite harmful to individuals and ends up creating problems that were not there before they got there. And so it's really important to recognize that and that this comes from this dynamic of power and control that we've been talking about. When I believe *I have the answer, I have the right way*, that is going to shift the way I interact one-on-one in my friendships. It's going to influence the way I function within my culture at large, but it's also going to determine how I see others outside of me, and then how I interact with those other people and what I determine they need in order to be more like me.

SIX

Seeing and Believing

It was 8 a.m. on a Thursday. Over the past few months, as part of my treatment plan following a car accident, I saw my physiotherapist before hopping on the bus to get to the university for a full day of classes. We did many things over the course of our work together, but I will never forget one moment in particular that taught me something about tending to my injuries that helped me to better understand my own experience of being human.

That day, we were working on a problem related to my shoulder. The physiotherapist was explaining to me that the tightness and restricted movement in my left shoulder originally made sense as I was recovering from the car accident. My muscles tightened up during the brace for impact, anticipating the coming blow. But now it was months after the accident, and my arm seemed to be stuck. Anything I did to rotate it created searing sensations in my arm and shoulder that made my chest tight. We had been working to loosen the tissues in a number of ways, but it seemed, again, like my body was stuck in defense mode.

My physiotherapist looked at me and told me we needed to work on getting things unstuck and that she would support my shoulder to move. She let me know it would hurt, but she would not be causing more damage. She reassured me that the pain of the motion would be part of my healing, even if it felt otherwise. We both took a deep breath, and with one of her hands on my arm and the other holding my hand, she manipulated my arm and shoulder in a few brief, swift, but gentle motions. The sensation could best be described as lightning striking a tree, slicing it down the middle. Lovingly, with a trustworthy sureness, she pulled my body out from the rigid, stuck defensive pattern it was in.

The searing continued for some time, as if my body was screaming, "This is not safe! Last time I was this free I got injured. I'm not ready to move like I used to." I continued to rehearse these movements on my own, but some of the old stuckness would creep back in. When I would go back for another treatment, the physiotherapist would continue to remind my body of other ways of moving that it had forgotten were possible. She seemed more sure of the goodness of my body and my ability to adapt and repair than I was. Seeing her sureness and feeling her competence made me feel safe and allowed me to tolerate the discomfort that came with undoing the ways I had learned to protect myself. She reminded me that my mind-body system knew how to heal under the right conditions, with the right support, and that sometimes there are aching, pain, and discomfort in stretching, but, especially with her by my side, the pain could be different from the original injury.

When I think of healing as an ideal, I imagine the sick days I had as a child where I would watch movies all day with a bottle tucked against my belly. The picture is of rest, ease, passive allowing, stillness, and being nurtured. Sometimes healing is gentle, giving our bodies time to rest and receive the care we so desperately need. But as I see it lived out day to day in my work with my patients, and in my own journey, our healing is often characterized by uncomfortable, bordering on painful, feelings. Healing is the grief of realizing how much time we spent believing things that hurt us. It is the anger we were never allowed to feel that still registers in our bodies as off-limits and untrustworthy. It is wading through our past to uncover just how deep the story goes. It is visceral fury at the system that bred all the hurt as well as enormous sadness that we perpetuated that harm. It is searing ache when we finally allow nurturing from another person after having been without for so long, the fear of what will happen when we let all parts of us be seen, and the excruciating discomfort of slowly trying to trust ourselves again while simultaneously expecting that doing so will get us punished. It is trying something old but in a different way, or trying something new and realizing that new things take practice and that uncomfortable sensations are part of our growth. It is the raw vulnerability of letting the painful places be witnessed and tended to.

I tell you all this because we are moving into the territory of healing and recovery. I really want healing to feel good, like we're all curled up on the couch watching a movie and eating popcorn together. When spiritual trauma has constricted access to and expression of self, one of the goals guiding our healing is that we be more fully ourselves. When we are less constricted, we are more able to experience pleasure and be in the right now. The goal is that we are better able to trust our goodness and the ease and safety of being in the present moment. We do all this to more deeply take in the love that is available to us and to learn how to calm ourselves down when we feel agitated. We are also making room for our feelings without inhibiting or defending against them. Healing is building systems that make our bodies well, speaking up when something isn't right, and knowing that our feelings can be listened to and learned from.

On the road to all these good things is often some discomfort. The process of healing sometimes requires looking at the thing we feel afraid to look at; other times healing is getting what we didn't get back then when we needed it; still other times healing is doing what we need to do so that we can set our defenses down and experience ourselves as a mind and body that are good, valuable, and worthy of love. Especially when we have come from a background of black-and-white thinking, healing is allowing ourselves to live in the complexity of knowing we will forever be grieving but can remake ourselves here in the midst of it.

If trauma fragments or fractures, then healing means piecing back together the parts that were shattered. Where there was disconnection, there can be connection; where there was powerlessness, there can be agency; where there was fear, there can be love; where we had to become hypervigilant and obsessive about what is to come, there can be a future so mysteriously hopeful that we can be fully present in the now; where we had to be perfect to feel lovable or good enough, it means allowing ourselves to radically accept ourselves as being lovable and valuable even as we grow and make mistakes. Healing is the journey we take to become whole, over time putting back together what was fragmented. In the case of spiritual trauma, healing is often the journey to remember that we were always whole, right from the beginning, despite what we were told otherwise.

The Words We Use for Healing

Before we get into the practicalities of healing from spiritual trauma, I want to spend some time contextualizing the conversation about healing. This is important when one of the insidious and wounding mechanisms of spiritual trauma occurs through convincing you of your brokenness and the need for healing in a specific way.

I believe this warrants, to start, some commentary about the word *healing* itself. There is some debate within the community of folks who have lived through and theorized about trauma on whether *healing* is appropriate to describe what could, should, or might happen after trauma. Especially in light of the assumption within some spiritual communities of healing being total and miraculous restoration to a prior state, the word has come to seem synonymous with fixing, curing, or erasing. The word *healing* seems to be haunted by the language of *healed*, where a definitive action and endpoint have occurred—leaving no trace of what happened before. Everything we experience, both the beautiful and the traumatic, shapes and changes us in some way. So returning to a prior state is not possible, especially when the injuries strike to the core of who we are. The very essence of trauma is that something has been altered inside us and shifted our sense of self and orientation to the world.

For this reason, some people choose not to use the word *healing* at all, or caution against using it as a promise of what is to come. Judith Herman uses the word *recovery* to identify the process by which the power and connection rightfully embodied by the survivor are reinstated.[1] However, at times even *recovery* can seem fraught, perhaps implying that something can be recovered, which may in fact not be the case.

The word *remaking* has been used by Karen O'Donnell and Katie Cross.[2] It comes from the trauma survivor community

153

itself, suggesting that what happens after trauma is the recon-struction of the self, an active and creative process that may take place over a lifetime. It is often nonlinear and complex and requires new meaning-making structures, stories, and interpretations of what happened. A person's sense of self, and often their relationships, needs to be built and rebuilt continuously.

Regardless of what words we use, we gain something by exploring what we mean when we say them. Shifting from the promise of an outcome to the language of a process by which we come to aliveness again following trauma allows us to better understand what is needed for that to happen, with recognition of the journey and the time that process takes. We can also weaponize words, using them to cause harm and create inhumane expectations that take us further from ourselves.

The word *healing* still holds something of value for me. As a trauma survivor who loves and works with other trauma survivors and witnesses their post-trauma process, healing captures something of the experience we have had and are continuing to have. It represents not an endpoint to chase after but what is unfolding inside us. To me, it is the unfolding and evolving process of bringing connection and love to the parts of ourselves that were fractured—in some cases to mend, in some cases to remake, and in some cases to build a quality of connection, aliveness, and stability that may not have been there before the thing we point to and call trauma. Healing is not going back to what was, but I have seen and felt how sometimes it includes something even richer than what was in the before—not easy, not effortless, but good.

Especially in light of the role of agency in the process of remaking that happens after trauma and knowing that my language might not work best for you as we begin to explore the underlying processes of living after trauma, I invite you to think of the words that best suit your understanding of what is happening now and what comes next.

Called to the Middle Space

Next, I want to be thoughtful about how to acknowledge where the hurt is and what caused it and provide some ideas on how to take steps toward healing—but without replicating the idea that you are a broken person and there is only one way to be restored.

At an earlier time in my life, if you had asked me what it meant to "witness" and why witnessing was so important for healing our world, I probably would have launched into a monologue about exactly what I thought it was by talking at you about any number of things. Should you have redirected me to your actual question, I would have told you that I thought witnessing was going into the broken world and telling people the good news. Without getting into the details of what I believed the good news was, specifically, witnessing was a form of telling, the spreading of information that could change someone's life, both now and in the future. It was something we were to offer to someone—or depending on who you ask and what it felt like, something we subjected them to. Either way, it was important, it was my responsibility, and it was something I was meant to offer my fellow humans to mend their brokenness.

The details are for another time, but in short, I haven't thought about witnessing at all, or like that, in a long time—until recently. When I read the book *Spirit and Trauma* by Shelly Rambo, I was immediately captivated by what I often sense is missing in both the academic world and the spiritual world, which I often bridge with my work. In Rambo's writing, there was a place for intellect, spirit, body, and context to all exist in the conversation about past, present, and future; grief and hope; life and death. When any of these elements are missing, the conversation is lacking the complexity needed to capture the human experience of trauma.

Rambo's description of trauma sounds very much like what we have already described in earlier chapters: "Trauma is described as an encounter with death. This encounter is not, however, a literal death but a way of describing a radical event or events that shatter all that one knows about the world and all the familiar ways of operating within it. A basic disconnection occurs from what one knows to be true and safe in the world."[3] Rambo then directs spiritual communities toward the in-between of surviving trauma with the not-yet integrated experiences of trauma living inside the body. She says spiritual communities (like churches) are called to this middle space where trauma is acknowledged but without glossing over the pain by pronouncing that nothing needs to hurt any more (which signals, as many of us likely felt, there is something wrong with you if you are still hurt, anxious, afraid, sad, ill, whatever). Instead, Rambo says healing is "about how we are with what stays, how we remain with what remains."[4] Interestingly, Judith Herman also uses *witness* to refer to the healing work of therapeutic relationships, in which the therapist must "bear witness to the crime."[5] When someone is reexperiencing the peak of their terror, rage, or grief as they process their trauma, I often lean in and say, "I'm seeing every bit of this, I am right here with you in this, and I'm not looking away."

Rambo's words remind me of what I tell my patients and what continues to be the most difficult part of healing for so many of us: *we have defined healing as something going away.* Instead, healing is the ability to attend to whatever is hurting, to turn toward where the injuries are and patiently, with courage and clarity, let them be loved, and eventually to love them ourselves. As they are. This means we are in relationship with the wounds we carry, even as they are wide open, telling the story for as long as necessary about how much pain we endured and what caused it. This does not mean we love what happened; rather, this is about our relationship with ourself.

While many people with spiritual trauma leave the religious contexts that caused the pain, they take with them the bypassing mechanisms—the skip-over-the-hurt-and-get-right-to-the-redemption strategies they learned so long ago. Healing spiritual trauma, whether inside the church or outside it, whether caused by our families or institutions or systems or a single person, is more about the process of how we can learn to be with it. Ultimately, this requires us to befriend the parts of ourselves that we might otherwise want to erase. Being in relationship with something means welcoming it, which is so different from the kind of banishing that we perhaps were previously taught was essential in order to prove we had healed. If trauma is about fragmentation, then healing is about connection.

For me, this has meant embodying the very principles I learned from the teachings of Jesus, who was known for hanging out with marginalized folks and people who had been socially devalued. I learned from this example to be in relationship with anything, anyone, any part of us that has been sent away, and I'm suggesting that healing means we do this both socially and in our own interior landscape. So instead of hating the anxiety we still feel when thinking about our time in that community, we turn toward the anxiety and ask it to tell us its story, believing it has something important to tell us and can be welcomed into our understanding of ourselves. In this way, healing occurs through relationship.

At some point, the journey of healing takes us beyond our connection with ourselves and into the connections between and around us. Here, we can redefine the word *witnessing*. Instead of defining it as talking at someone or passing on information, what if we restored the word *witness* to mean the process of fully seeing? I mean this not just in an observational way, where we objectively report what happens to someone else, but rather as a true encounter in which we see someone's experiences, what Jewish philosopher Martin Buber describes as the sacredness of an I–thou encounter. In this encounter, the other person is not an object to analyze, use, or fix but a life to be related to, rehumanized, and experienced for who they are, as they are. Witnessing demands that we really see where the pain is and that we don't look away from it, minimize it, explain it, pray it away, or pretend it was never there.

As Rambo suggests in her book, to really witness we must enter into the heart of someone's suffering. While we might wish to shy away from doing this or desire a formula to follow for engaging in this manner, either would turn the other person into an object. These are mechanisms to manage our own discomfort about a process that has no straightforward path. A term we like to use in the therapy world is *holding space*. It means remaining—eyes open, heart open—and seeing what has been unbearable to be with. This is the kind of witnessing our wounds need: a shared encounter to look at the places of pain with the eyes of love. This requires a see-er, someone with a loving gaze who bears witness, who undoes the aloneness of the injuries we sustained. And it asks the person who holds the pain to allow their wounds to be seen, to courageously show their injuries and feel the risk inherent in that—the fear of exposing the damaged part of oneself and risking further injury.

Healing trauma cannot happen without the presence of connection. It requires an integration of me within myself, me and you, and all of us together. As we take that line of thinking as far as it will go, we see that just like all the layers of fragmentation parallel one another, all the layers of connection parallel one another too. The disconnection inside me is tied to the disconnection in all my relationships. When we work to restore one relationship, we can borrow whatever works to mend that relationship and extend it to the others. When I bear witness to myself and my own inner experiences, doing so makes it easier for me not to turn away as you tell the truth about your pain. And that makes me want to look at what I do to all other living beings and systems and see how my behavior impacts them. I find that it is harder to use the earth like a thing after moving away from being used and using my own body like a thing. When I see what is inside me that is hard to look at and love, I find it easier to love your painful truths, and when you love the painful truths in me without looking away, I get the courage to do the same. It is then that I can love my neighbor as myself and love myself as my neighbor.

It is not in the way that I once thought, but witnessing is connected to the healing of the world after all.

Letting Our Trauma Be Seen

Before we get into inner witnessing—that is, holding a witness inside ourselves—I want to talk about what really being seen by others means and how it is important when it comes to trauma.

Within Western cultures, with their historically cognitive and individualistic Eurocentric worldviews, we have produced a method of understanding the person and their pain that centers the individual. The therapy models that are part of my profession have historically taken an androcentric, White, disembodied, pathologizing, and colonial perspective of the person and filtered our understanding of trauma and recovery through those lenses. As such, our understanding of trauma, and post-traumatic stress disorder (PTSD) specifically, tends to center the idea of the individual—their thoughts, their nervous system, their experiences and memories—while neglecting the importance of the social context of our pain and healing.

Following some important publications in the late 2000s, more theories about social models of healing PTSD started to emerge. Those theories led to more empirically valid ideas about how trauma and its healing are connected to what is happening in our social contexts. By this point in the book, it likely won't surprise you to read that our social contexts and how we are witnessed in our experiences profoundly impact both how we are able to process trauma and what our nervous systems code as traumatic.

Research of the past two decades has found that a lack of social support is one of the strongest predictors of how severe a person's trauma symptoms will be. The opposite is also true: consistent and high levels of social support shape a person's experience of mental and physical health. The uncontested research finding is that how people around us respond to our trauma has a dramatic impact on our well-being, our resilience to stress, and the psychobiological symptoms that follow our trauma.

Here are some other things to know about the social aspect of trauma healing. First, any trauma that we perceive as being caused by another person, as opposed to an event like an earthquake, results in more severe and long-lasting trauma responses. This has not shown up in the research data just yet, but my assumption is that in a religion or spiritual practice that is inherently relational, this idea of a "relationship" includes our understanding of a personal and relational God. If our injury is affiliated with someone we perceive to be everywhere and responsible for everything—the very template of all relating—our fear can generalize quickly to other relational and interpersonal dynamics.

The interpersonal piece is connected to the second point. There are huge benefits to disclosing our traumas, but when the trauma is interpersonal in nature, we struggle to trust other people and share our pain, especially if we have adopted the belief that we are to blame. If we are able to share our trauma with someone and they blame us, that creates another injury all its own. You can imagine how complicated this gets if we are courageous enough to tell our community that trauma has occurred in our church or with a leader or community group, and then we are blamed, told it didn't happen, or told that it was actually good and a part of our journey to be made holy.

Third, remember the pre-traumatic factors we talked about in chapter 4? Our attachment style—or the template of connection we learned in our earliest caregiving relationships—impacts how likely we are to share or not share. If our early attachments were unhealthy, we are less likely to feel like we belong in a social group and may not have as many people to tell about our experiences. Or we might be so desperate for the belonging we never got growing up that we will do whatever we can to belong, even if it means denying our trauma, going along with it, or dismissing our own reactions when we feel minimized by others.

Fourth, when we have a social place for talking about our trauma, this not only softens the response our bodies have to the trauma but also boosts our mental and physical health. So you can imagine how in a faith or family context where we experienced a spiritual trauma, a subsequent confrontation that forces us to leave the group will leave us not only trau-matized but also lacking a social network for processing it. This is a serious wound in itself. When religious systems are closed and prohibit people from building connections outside the religious community, they are left with nowhere to turn.

Fifth, the severity of our trauma symptoms depends on how heard and supported we feel by others when we tell them what happened. If someone shares with you about their trauma, here are some questions you should ask yourself: How do I help them feel understood? How can I acknowledge what happened? Do they feel accepted, believed, and emotionally safe with me? A person's ability to answer yes to these ques-tions can change whether they are likely to receive a PTSD diagnosis following a trauma. A system of support allows the stress that lives in their body following the awfulness of what happened to be processed and integrated.

Not everyone with trauma will receive a PTSD diagnosis. In some cases, this is because of barriers to diagnosis and also the limitations and specificity of diagnostic criteria. So diagnostic criteria aside, it's important to note that social support and acknowledgment drastically improve a person's quality of life for a number of reasons. Extrapolating this to the context of spiritual trauma, many people will not get the social support they need, and worse, they will likely be blamed, ignored, or misunderstood. While this often happens inside the religious group, it can also happen outside religious contexts. People unfamiliar with the patterns of control, manipulation, coer-cion, and power exercised in systems causing spiritual trauma might be confused about how a person could stay in a context that was causing them harm. Well-meaning friends, family members, or even therapists—especially those with their own unexamined spiritual trauma—might not know how to say "I believe you," "It wasn't your fault," or "Of course you stayed.

You were told this was your family and you would suffer for eternity if you didn't do what they asked." These wounds are real and lasting. They can heal, but it is harder for that to happen when the wounds are invisible to others.

At their best, spiritual communities create spaces where people can truly be seen and accompanied through the aftermath of trauma. Places like this can create rich foundations of belonging and connection that serve as protection against traumas that might come in the future. At their worst, spiritual communities demand exclusivity of time, service, money, and relationship in a way that renders a person wounded in many ways if they ever exit the abusive system. These places leave people feeling disconnected, ostracized, and shamed at a time when they need connection the most. Although there are many reasons why individuals may struggle with mental health challenges after leaving an abusive religious or spiritual community, the significance of compounding loneliness on top of unprocessed trauma cannot be overstated. Additionally, if a person was raised in an environment with distorted perceptions of interpersonal boundaries (for example, excessively vulnerable sharing with others when trust has not been earned), this can leave a person without the skills to navigate relationships with others on the "outside."

Being witnessed is foundational to our ability to know that trauma is over and to begin to heal. We are relational, so our pain needs to be held tenderly, with engagement, care, and presence, as we speak about it. In the therapy world, we talk about it as "feeling felt." And whether we choose to tell our story or not, we deserve spaces where we are felt and known and trust that we are believed.

While it's essential to center the experience of the person who has lived the trauma, we also need to explore how we build relationships and communities where we can bear witness lovingly, skillfully, and without feeling overwhelmed ourselves. When we are overwhelmed and don't know how to hold what we are witnessing, we're tempted to shut the other person down or take too much on ourselves in order to "fix" them. This moves us out of witnessing and into solving or saving. Ironically, doing so creates a power dynamic whereby the person with the trauma becomes a problem to be solved so we can resolve our own distress. By contrast, the witnessing I am talking about means to be with and really see the reality of what happened. Witnessing asks us to slow down, to be present, to notice our own reactions, to be aware of our own boundaries, and to know when and how to authentically say, "Tell me more about what that was like for you" or "I believe you, and that should have never happened" or "How is that living in you now?" It also asks us to acknowledge when we're incapable of handling certain types of information. We might need to say, "This is so important. I want you to get the care you need to help your body know that this is over, but I'm not able to do that in the way you deserve. I want to help find someone for you to talk to."

More often than not, witnessing just means that when someone shares we respond with care. We can offer an appropriate response: "I'm so glad you're telling me" or "What happened was not okay" or "I don't understand all of that, but I want to, and I'm going to learn more so that I can support you in ways that help you." Saying these things would be easier if we practiced them regularly and heard them ourselves. Think back to what we covered on attachment and family of origin. If others consistently minimized our pain when we shared it, we won't have the body memory of having our feelings validated and won't always know how to validate others. But learning how to do that as witnesses is our job if we wish to build a culture where people can heal.

You might be catching on to this, but becoming people who can witness also means we put our phones down, look for the people on the margins of the community, build relationships, take risks to be vulnerable, and do our own work to explore what gets in the way of our ability to do this. That is easier said than done when our social contexts keep us busy, numb, avoiding, overscheduled, or overworked in order to survive in increasingly expensive cities. It is a lot to try to build healthy connections when we have so much working against us. But I also have this niggling feeling that relationship—the I–thou encounter that happens when we are witnessing and being witnessed—is powerful enough that it can slowly upset the systems that dehumanize us. Seeing and being seen are *rehu-manizing*. Feeling felt inherently connects us back to ourselves and to each other.

Darryl W. Stephens says that bearing witness is a spiritu-ally significant form of action we can take as communities in response to trauma.[6] It is a form of social justice to be present to one another in moments of pain. We can be for one another the face of love, the enfleshed Spirit of interconnectedness, looking into the eyes of a person who is hurting and saying with our attention and presence that Love, the Holy, is right here and cares about you. This is my own lens. If it doesn't fit for you or feels painful, you might consider it this way: seeing one another like this is an actualization of the ideal, a bringing into the here and now the qualities of goodness that we might have been told are only out there, or a fantasy, or beyond our reach. It is a way of restoring the quality of with-ness or right relationship that repairs the fractures in our relational systems and ecosystems. It is the relational landscape that gives rise to the capacity for healing that lives within and between us.

When our religious systems slowly shove to the outskirts the people who carry wounds, who don't comply, who can't seem to perform well on the moral and behavioral tightrope, we need to look for systems that surround us at the broken places. This means not only refusing to ignore the pain but also allowing it to inform the way we respond, love, support, and intervene. It might even mean we need to create communities specifically designed around how to best support the folks who are living with trauma. In doing so, we might find we build better and more beautiful communities where we all can heal.

I have learned through working with folks who have trauma how to love better, how to be more present. They have taught me what safety is. I believe traumatized people not only carry perseverance inside them but also have a powerful and prophetic message for our systems about what does not work and the way forward for healing. Their pain deserves to be witnessed because it teaches us. The social nature of trauma healing benefits everyone because when a person has trauma and can be held in community, they are better for it, but we are also *all* better for it. Our own fragmenting is reversed and the pain in our communal bodies healed.

While I'm talking here about witnessing, or bearing witness, I want to be clear that telling our stories and the truth about what we have been through lies on a continuum. There are multiple layers of sharing, and true connection is most available when the person sharing and the person witnessing are matched and consenting in their level of capacity. That means when we are the person with the trauma, it is important that we ask the person we want to tell our story to if they have the space to hear what we have to say and that we respect their boundaries. When we are the person holding space, we are aware of what we are capable of, what skills we have, what our energy level is, and what we might be able to freely offer to the other person.

The practice of letting ourselves be seen can be challenging, especially if we haven't been believed in the past or are afraid of judgment. This fear often has to do with our early experiences growing up. So we might ask a person if they are able to listen, both as a way of honoring them and as a way of gauging whether they are a person we can trust. We might also realize that sharing only a part of what has happened or giving only a few rough details without much else can sometimes be harder than telling them nothing or revealing everything.

Telling the truth can sometimes include sharing the details of our experience with a qualified professional with whom we have built trust. But more often, telling the truth can be as simple as saying, "I've experienced a kind of spiritual wounding that leaves me feeling afraid all the time, and I'm coming to terms with how deep that wounding goes. I think I'm realizing it was a form of trauma, and calling it such has me feeling confused, afraid, angry, and alone." As a trauma expert, I often inform people in the first session that telling their story isn't actually something we get to right away. Telling their story can very easily lead to a reliving for them as they talk about the details and sort through what happened, something they are not yet ready to experience. Having boundaries on what we share can actually be part of the healing itself, especially given the boundary violations that often occur in spiritual environments where people are expected to share intimate details about their lives without any relational safety or assurances of confidentiality. As the motto of trauma work in the therapy world goes, we need to slow down to speed up.

Your Goodness Can't Be Taken Away

As I've alluded to, bearing witness to one another is easier when we have felt someone be a witness for us. The skills of attuning are transferable. This leads us to the concept of *inner witnessing*. I want to say upfront that we'll dive more deeply into this in the next chapter and that the skills related to it can take a while to practice. If we were told that the inner critic was the voice of God, it can take a long time to really believe an inner nurturer exists, can be trusted, and is actually a voice of our own. So think of this as a door I'm opening that you are invited to walk through over and over.

Inner witnessing, or witnessing ourselves, might sound strange unless you remember that we talk to ourselves all the time. We criticize ourselves, judge ourselves, laugh at ourselves, negotiate internally, and have inner conflict. One part of us is relieved to leave the party, while the other part of us wants to stay. The idea of multiple parts of us, all existing inside of who we are as a person, has been around for a long time. Carol Gilligan and the women at the Stone Center started talking about the multiplicity of the self in the 1980s as a feminist and intersectional way of thinking about our inner world, and similar ideas have been popularized through the Internal Family Systems therapy model.[7] They posited that our inner worlds (our thoughts, feelings, actions, and reactions) are more like a band playing together than a concert pianist playing on their own. Having different instruments or "voices" allows us to navigate the world with safety, power, connection, and our own unique expression. When the band is playing the same song—or the choir is singing in harmony—it sounds and feels good to be us. But more often than not, the different voices in the choir are singing different songs: one is singing the song that we were taught to sing growing up in our family; one is singing a song imprinted on us by our culture; one is humming the melody of that old boyfriend or gym coach; one is belting out the song that is sung by the person in the room with the most power; one is humming along with the song of resistance; one is singing the song of fear from when we were really hurt and alone. And all of this is happening inside our mind simultaneously.

In the midst of all those voices and songs is a part of you that knows how to witness. This is the part of you that comes out when you feel like the very best version of yourself: strong and patient, loving and wise, clear and communicative, courageous and resilient. Even if that part feels pushed to the very back of the choir, I know this to be true: it exists and cannot be taken from you—especially if you have survived trauma. This wise, most you-est you is there, is yours, and can never be destroyed. As I understand it, this is the divine spark in you that is in us all, written into our DNA. It is spirit that is both in us and is us, right here, in our bodies and breathing lungs, right now. If this language doesn't work for you, think of it as your core self, the valuable aliveness each of us is born with as a human. This is the self inside you that shows up when someone you love is hurting and you want to reach toward them to make it better. It is the self that has the idea to do something kind for someone else or wants to try again at something hard because there might be a chance it could be different this time. It is the self that makes something, generates ideas, and puts more of you into the world.

Imagine the chorus of voices singing inside you. When I picture this, sometimes it's with tea and baked goods set out on a table in a location that feels homey—like someone put thought into this and the intention was caring. Even if the room is filled with loud voices, allow yourself to know that your core self, the part of you capable of bearing witness, is in that room. You might even be able to imagine that the self who is looking at the room, seeing all the other parts, is the core self, the witness. In this situation, you would see through the sea and chaos of noise and notice the self who carries the pain of what has happened. And maybe if the other parts would allow you to get through, you would sit with this part, the one in pain, and say, "I want to know your story." Or maybe, if that does not yet feel quite true, "I hope one day be able to know your story, and I'm so sorry that you have been here all along hurting, and I haven't been able to find my way to you."

I could go on, and there will be an opportunity for us to do this more later in the book. But for now, please hear these three things: (1) trauma asks for a witness as part of its healing; (2) we can be the witness to others, but we too deserve a witness ourselves; and (3) sometimes the witness is us, for us, inside ourselves.

Loving Our Selves Who Lived Through Trauma

My friend Kurt leads a beautiful and hopeful faith community in Portland, Oregon. A few years ago we were having a conversation about what life felt like for me this side of eating disorder recovery. Having heard what I said, he said back to me to clarify, "So are you saying that you love your mental illness because it allowed you to be here?" He was trying to help me articulate what I thought about my own healing and integration. I wasn't quite sure what I was trying to say, but his words held up a mirror to help me see what I was hinting at.

I don't quite know how to articulate it, but the conversation with Kurt got me thinking about who I was all those years ago. I love who I am now, I love my present and my future, and so much of that has to do with being able to be with other people in the way that I experienced when I was in the most painful places in my own journey. I believe my current contentment comes from having looked at painful parts of my past and loving the versions of myself who lived through it all. I'm not endorsing that trauma, nor would I want the pain I endured for anyone else, but I'm able now to look at my younger self with love. I can also look with appreciation at the parts of myself that did their very best to cope and survive, even if those were not the best choices of how to manage. I can look back now and see how I was doing my very best. In other words, the present me that I am so grateful for is connected to a past. I can't just edit out the parts of my past that I don't like and assume that I would still be the same person I am today.

From this vantage point in my life, I can see that the pain inside me wasn't the problem; rather, it was the way my body was telling the truth about the world, about the things that happened to me, about what was needed but I never got. Seeing it this way allowed me to change my relationship to the pain in a way that made it more tolerable to be with, which ultimately is what helped move my healing forward. It was like the pain was a kind of breaking open, the voice of a prophet. When I learned to turn toward it, it could be transformed into a life being born inside me that looks like vision and feels like love.

I do not believe we need pain to grow or that we are fundamentally broken and in need of saving to become who we are supposed to be. But I do wonder if part of what makes spiritual trauma so difficult, so intractable in its healing, is not the wounds but that we don't know how to be with them individually or culturally. When pain happens, we are left alone with it, or it's covered up, or we feel shame that it exists at all and want to disappear in a way that means the pain can't get the witnessing it needs. In the wise words of Bayo Akomolafe, offering us a cultural critique, "What if the ways we respond to the crisis are part of the crisis?"[8]

I wonder what would happen if we knew how to be with the pain of the trauma instead of trying to manage it away? What if we knew that it would not kill us to feel the feelings that are supposed to happen when we have been hurt and that on the other side we would still exist and would know something more about ourselves, the world, how to be in it, and how to help others be in it?

This is a potential that exists for all of us. Even if this seems far away, try it on this way. It is one of the many options in the infinite options in the universe of how things could go. If we are able to find the ability to look back on what happened and make meaning of it, maybe we can find the ability to make some kind of living here and now in spite of the trauma. If that feels too hard, maybe what is available is that we hold the possibility that someone out there believes that a younger version of us was doing the best we could, and they want to turn toward who we were, even if only to let us know they have been there too. Or maybe we start with a "What if . . . ?" What if, by really bearing witness to our trauma and feeling the grief of it all as we process through it, the capacity to endure, remain, and feel even more of ourselves was revealed? I have seen that when we get closer to believing this that we soften the urge to turn away from pain and look with the eyes of one who really understands, bearing witness to the pain but seeing that it changes us all in the process.

Shelly Rambo writes that "attempting to map the experiences of trauma comes from my conviction that our lives are inextricably bound together. Given what we know about the historical dimensions of trauma, no one remains untouched by overwhelming violence. Trauma becomes not simply a detour on the map of faith but, rather, a significant reworking of the entire map."[9] For those of you who have spiritual trauma, your healing gets to look the way that you need it to look. This might mean leaving the context, relationship, community, or religion where the harm happened. Finding safety, renarrating your past, allowing for the grief of what happened to clean out a space inside you that hopes for something more: all of this will happen when you are able to begin to name what happened and know that your trauma deserves to be witnessed. Until that happens, know that I believe your body deserves to be at rest.

Now, to the institutions, the systems, the communities, and the leaders responsible for the trauma—and the people who benefit from them or who have been bystanders to the harm—we need to listen to the voices and stories of the traumatized. Doing this is vital to helping us understand more about what is hurting people and actually doing the very thing we are called to do in the world, which is to bear witness to them and extend love and care. Witnessing is fundamentally different from spiritually bypassing. Those within these systems need to open their eyes to the wounds they have caused and know that the people they have wounded have something important to say about what has gone awry. When the map of a spiritual community causes damage to the people it is claiming to love, it needs to be reworked.

Giving Up Control

In the last phase of my formal eating disorder treatment, I remember sitting across from my therapist. She was in a partially reclining chair, her notebook out and pen poised, and asked me about what recovery looked like for me. Up until then I had never really had to define it. I was cycled through a system in which people told me what they expected of my eating, my weight, my body, my thinking. I didn't have to find my voice or know what I wanted; I just had to do what I was told.

I remember sharing about my plan to do recovery the right way: not a trace of the eating disorder left, none of it detectible to anyone else or myself. Instead of the eating disorder being in control of my life, I would be. I went on with a naive rigidity masquerading as optimism and devotion to health as I described how this version of recovery was something I was committed to.

I don't remember the details of how we got from that idea to where we ended up in the session, but I remember there were some questions, I had a click of insight and recognition, and then there was a gentle unraveling. Somewhere between the therapist's skillful questions and my knack for process-based thinking, I realized I was approaching recovery in the same way I had lived when I developed my eating disorder. Here are some words and phrases that describe what I felt was required:

- perfection
- control
- achievement (of the unachievable)
- black-and-white thinking
- rigidity
- going it alone

This is something so many of us do in our attempts to change things: we try to manage the healing in a way that perpetuates what caused the hurt. I was doing that with my eating disorder. I was trying to live and die by what I did with my eating and food; only this time, the obsessively restrictive goal would be my perfect recovery. It was in recognizing that piece of insight that I saw both the way out and how far I had to go. And somehow, I also started to feel the edges of *that* story dissolve, the one about being on a trajectory with a start point and an end point, where the start was the brokenness and the end was glowing, awakened wholeness. I feel myself taking a deep exhale even as I write this, giving myself the permission to see I don't have to be somewhere else to be healed and acknowledging the awareness that there is always more to know, always more I can't see, no matter where I'm positioned.

That session reminded me that growing is meant to be good and challenging and easy and hard and beautiful and uniquely mine—somehow all together. I realized I needed to have softness and flexibility in my definition of recovery. Embracing this antidote to perfectionism signified that something had shifted in me. I needed my recovery to encompass other elements of my life, things that had nothing to do with eating or weight or mental illness or treatment. Being able to see the goal of working on my friendships and going back to school as part of my recovery would tell me that my recovery was underway already. Interestingly, and most perplexingly, allowing my eating disorder to be peripherally in my life without my own judgment, anxiety, or self-scrutiny was for me also ultimately the mark of my recovery. It was when I no longer overanalyzed my recovery, no longer lived my life by measuring and looking for control in the same way I had in my eating disorder, that I knew I was in recovery.

◆ ◆ ◆

We can't heal from control by controlling what healing looks like. We won't mend the wounds of our perfectionism by trying to do so perfectly. We will still be missing something we need if we try to shame ourselves out of shame.

In many cases, the very definition of healing, the marker that we are well on the road to recovery, is being able to accept ourselves exactly where we are.

· PRACTICE ·
Inner Witnessing

The need to be seen and accompanied in the big moments in life, the painful feelings, the beautiful discoveries, is core to our experience of being human. It allows us to integrate and make meaning, process the intensity of the feeling that would otherwise live on in our nervous systems, and feel our aloneness undone through the presence of the loving gaze of another. Although experiencing this with others is ideal, sometimes letting others in to see our inner world is too intolerable, or there is no one around in a moment when we need to be seen. So here is a practice for inner witnessing. My recommendation is that you try this here and now but also in the days coming—in a moment that seems to hold the tiniest little blip of emotion. Those are the moments when we build the stamina and strength to be able to hold the bigger experiences.

You might start by settling your body and bringing to mind someone you love. Perhaps you even have a memory of them or photo in your mind. As you hold them in your mind, notice how you feel toward them. Notice how those feelings move in your body right now (perhaps a swelling heart, deep sigh, settling shoulders, or smile on your face). Now bring to mind the place in their heart that holds pain. You might see it, or you might just know that it is there, somewhere inside—maybe small, maybe of great depth and density. Imagine how you might look on this place inside them, even before you say or do anything else. Then imagine what you might say directly to this place of pain. Try one of the following:

- I am here with you.
- I love you.
- Show me where it hurts.
- I believe it is that awful.

You might stop there, but if you want to go further, imagine that inside of witnessing the person you love, you are now seeing the part of you holding *your* pain. Try saying those things again, noticing how much you can tolerate. You also might need to say, "I will come back for you" or "I want to come back for you, and I am going to go away and build the sturdiness that you deserve; then I will return, and I might bring someone else to help me love you in the way you deserve."

If you can't imagine this for yourself, perhaps imagine someone else, maybe even me, Hillary, being the loving witness, offering this to the you who holds pain.

Alison Cook and J.S. Park on Healing

Alison and J.S. have been introduced in previous chapters. Here is more from them on the topic of healing from spiritual and religious trauma.

Alison

Of number one importance for healing our wounds is awareness. We tend to want to fix it. We want to get intellectual, tell ourselves what's true. But that doesn't get to the wound. So always, always is that awareness of *I might not know what love really feels like. I might not know what it feels like to be seen, to be held.* And there's grief involved in that. But step one is just that acknowledgment and to move toward that curiosity, and realizing, *Oh my goodness, it's not my fault.* We try to remove the shame from it, because a lot of times shame gets in here. And just okay, here we go. You know, and then that's the beginning. So then there's a healing process as with any trauma. But number one is that acknowledgment, that awareness.

We have to begin to then notice and honor the cues. What are the cues my body is telling me? What are the cues my emotions are telling me? When I'm with this person or in this space, whether it's a church or a faith community or with a parent, where I was taught this was love but boy my body does not experience this as love. Or my emotions are telling me I feel unsafe. Noticing, honoring, validating. Again, there's this peeling back the onion, that curiosity, you know, so that's the pre-work. And then beginning to notice.

I always talk to my clients about Where do you feel safe? What makes you feel alive? What brings you joy, love, a sense of presence? And they're always surprised at what that looks like. Sometimes it's so different from what they thought it should look like. It might have been a grandparent. It might have been a random friend who didn't even share a faith system, but just someone about whom they were able to say, "I just felt safe with that person." Okay, great. So your body understands, your soul got a glimpse there, so let's talk about that. Let's move toward that. There's so much to this. But then last, I would say, as folks are ready and want to, we can begin to disentangle some of the messages on a more cognitive level about what God is like, or what love means, or what kindness is. We can begin to disentangle some of what we were shown from what we want to believe to be true, what we actually believe to be true, and then rebuild spiritual practices around what we've now taught ourselves through those experiences—those new experiences of what safety actually feels like inside our bodies, inside our souls.

I think of Jesus's words about causing the little ones to stumble and just how precious those young ones inside us are. We all have these prior versions of ourselves inside us, and those young parts of us are precious too. Those young ones are precious and they're worthy. Those young ones inside each of us are worth pursuing, bearing witness to the pain and re-creating those safe connections, those safe experiences. It's so amazing to me that our bodies and souls are actually designed to heal in the context of loving compassion.

It's a beautiful thing. I know in your work as well we get to be privy to that. And it's amazing. It is indeed holy ground. It is beautiful and it can be a process, but I've seen it so many times. We encourage people not to give up hope.

I had a medical crisis two years ago, and I'm like, *Wow, my body knows what to do.* My body knows how to send the right aspects of itself to mend the wound. It knows how to send the right clotting mechanisms to heal that cut. And our souls are no different in the context we need. And sometimes, when there's a deep gash, we have to go to the emergency room and we need a surgeon to get in there and delicately bring those tissues back together. It's the same with our souls. Some wounds to the soul—with a little bit of care and a little bit of a Band-Aid—we can heal on our own. And some wounds to the soul require deep surgery, deep tissue surgery. But either way that soul is wired and designed with a bent toward healing.

Joon

Just as bad theology and bad leaders are the origin of spiritual trauma, I think healing theology and guides who come alongside—and cheer you on and root for you and reflect the goodness of God—offer a healing way forward. People who are in the work of dismantling and undoing systemic abuse, they're also so much a part of feeling secure and knowing that there are people who are not just alongside you but in those systems and around those systems doing the work to undo it.

The kind of theology that for me is healing is when it's . . . I don't know another word for this besides *fuzzy*. When it's not so certain, when there's ambiguity around it, there's the ability to ask questions and the ability to say this is not going to resolve.

There's no spiritual bow tie to this. There is no eschatology to this.

I am in pain. This illness is hurting me. I am mad at God, and there is no landing pad for me. Not everything is going to resolve. This storm is not going to pass. You know, theology allows us to say that. And if you look in the Psalms, if you look at the wrestling within Judaism, if you look at the sorrow and anguish of the Korean concept of *haan*, there is so much freedom and movement in being able to freely express all the pain and hurt that the world can bring upon us.

The way to heal spiritual trauma is to know that the thing that happened wasn't my fault, and it's not because God hates me. And that thing that happened, it's not because I somehow attracted it to myself or that somehow I was "asking for it." And it's not some sort of moral retribution at some cosmic level. Evil exists, unfortunately. Evil systems that are often unintentional and just built on apathy can cause trauma. But the spiritual narrative around that—about it not being my fault, it not making me lesser, it not shaping my moral identity and value—that's such an important thing to learn. And to unlearn the ideas of cause and effect of supernatural imposition of the order: How do I undo that certainty and leave it to ambiguity and then be okay with that ambiguity?

If I can put one word around healing, it is *expansiveness*. In my chaplain residency, which was a yearlong program after a six-month internship, I lost my faith for a season. And I lost my faith because I was seeing so much suffering. My theology was not enough to hold me through it. And thank God for my supervisor. She sat me down, drew a box, and said, "This was your faith." And then she drew another box that had a broken edge, and she said, "Now here is your faith with this broken edge." And then she kind of drew a third box, but like sort of, you know, not a box. She said, "This is where you may end up, this expanded, open box. We don't know where you're going to land, but this is what it's going to be. And it'll keep changing." What she gave me was room and expansiveness to grow.

And thank God for my supervisor, who was such a guide through that process of being able to say, "It's okay that your faith is broken. But what you're going to see on the other end, it may be no faith at all, it may be something completely different. But whatever that is, feel free to have the room to grow into it."

For those experiencing spiritual trauma, it's like their whole lives they may have been told this is the way that God works. God fits in this box, and you cannot go outside that box. But once we're given permission, once we're given the grace and the love and the kindness and compassion to ask questions and to look at suffering, then we can say, "You know what, my box isn't working for this." My box isn't working for the hurt that I'm experiencing. My box isn't working for this illness, for my divorce. It's not working for my parenting. It's not working for my fight against systemic injustices. I'm having to maintain this box, and it's keeping me in prison. But my supervisor gave me that permission to say, "It's okay that you feel this way. And on the other end, wherever you land, I'm going to be with you." That was the expansiveness that I needed to grow.

SEVEN

Mending and Meaning

Several years ago, on a cool November night in Ojai, California, I was sitting in a cedar hot tub late at night staring up at the moon. It was so bright that the middle of the night almost looked like dawn. With the exception of soft shadows cast under nearby trees, it seemed like I could see everything. I was trying to integrate an experience I had just had, one that would come to be one of the most profound experiences of my life. In a way I never had before, I had come face-to-face with myself, and I both saw and felt my own goodness. Prior to that moment, my core sense of innate goodness was only a rumor that I was desperate to believe was true.

I kept breathing and trying to memorize the moment, the feeling. What I knew now was what I had always hoped for. As the space opened up in my chest with each breath, I felt fear begin to creep in, whispering from my sternum, *What if I forget? What if I can't remember this forever?* I sensed in that moment what I had experienced was at once enormous and unbreakable but also fragile. I wanted so badly to put a fence around it, to keep it immortal.

I remember wanting to scrape the surface of the earth to collect enough dust under my fingernails that the moment would stay forever. And then the moon caught my eye, almost like a grandmother looking down on me. I imagined her saying with a wise and steady voice, "I am the same moon who has seen you in every moment of agony, and I saw this too. Anytime you forget, look at me, and I will remind you that what happened here today was real. I will keep the memory of this alive for you."

That day, the moon and I made a pact. And since that day, I have found myself often sitting beneath her, a wise teacher I have much to learn from, the edges of her robe of light touching my toes. On some nights, I look up and feel the moon, almost full, illuminating my face with its glow, and I am brought back to that night when I met my essence and it was good. On other nights, when the moon is barely visible, I am reminded that sometimes I might seem like only a slice of myself—most of my brightness hidden away as if covered by a shadow yet still there even if unseen by myself or others.

Not long after this experience, my friend Melaney shared with me that the moon reminds us that no matter what phase we are in, we are always whole. And day after day, which turned into month after month, which has quickly become years now of watching the moon, I have found so much resonance between the cycles of the moon and our cycles of living. This has taught me much about healing too: our paths are not so much linear to a destination with a fixed point but circular, reflecting ebb and flow.

Three Stages of Healing

The moon in its wholeness and its changing has been an existential compass for me, a reminder of what is coming, of where

I have been. It has also normalized the process of healing as both believing my wholeness to be constant and allowing for dynamism and change. When healing feels disorienting—our identities in crisis and our experiences confusing—we can look at nature and see how the moon, like the seasons and the tides and so many other cycles in nature, offer help in orienting us within the wider world, which can otherwise seem chaotic and disorderly. I want to introduce a theoretical framework to act as another sort of compass when things feel disorganized on the journey of healing.

I briefly touched on the ideas of Judith Herman, the influential psychiatrist in the field of trauma studies, in the previous chapter. She has proposed three stages for healing that can guide our understanding of the path to recovery in the therapeutic journey toward integration.

The first stage, according to Herman, is *safety*. This means building a healing relationship in the here and now and making intolerable feelings bearable through connection with others. In the world of spiritual trauma, sometimes this means getting out of the environment or relationship that caused the trauma, or getting away from anything that reminds the person's body of the trauma. Sometimes getting away is for a season; sometimes it is forever. But the body needs to know that what happened is over and have space to heal from it without the wounds being reopened.

In therapy this can be the longest and most difficult phase, especially when a person has learned that others can't be trusted or that therapy is dangerous and psychology is too "worldly" or when a leader of some sort was the one doing the hurting. Often, relationship is at the center of creating safety, and the tool in the relationship is the authentic empathy of the person who is witnessing or caring. Empathy, when therapeutic, is real. It's a person caring for another person and creating an environment that supports and centers that person's experience.

When one of the ways we were injured was by being fragmented from our body and believing our body is dangerous, we often need to do the work of coming in contact with the body. Because the process of relating to our bodies is not so different from relating to others, we can often borrow from the safety we find in connection with others to begin to turn toward our body and the sensations, memories, and emotions that live there. Alternately, sometimes it is creating a safe, attuned, and empathic relationship with our bodily self that creates the courage to begin to trust others. Finding safety in our body may be as painful and as simple as saying (as a whole, as well as the sensations, memories, and emotions within), "I'm sorry you were ever told you were bad. Even when it's hard to do so, I want to learn to listen to you tell the story of what we have lived through, and offer you the care and honoring you deserve."

Herman's second stage is reconstructing the narrative, processing memories of the trauma, and *allowing grief* about what happened. Grief can occur when our bodies actually believe that we are outside the trauma enough to see it with fresh eyes. Instead of feeling like it is still happening, we can look at it, believe it happened, know it is over, and feel the agony and pain that it happened at all. This can feel counterintuitive, because we might think that we would feel relief when we are safe. But, especially with trauma that is tangled in layers and systems and relationships and beliefs, we often can't see the trauma clearly; we know only that we feel horrible or afraid and that something has to change. It is when we feel safe that we can look back on the memories of what happened and see them as others see them, with a survivor's eyes.

Sometimes this involves the active work of processing using trauma therapies like Eye Movement Desensitization and Reprocessing (EMDR), Somatic Experiencing (SE), Accelerated Experiential Dynamic Psychotherapy (AEDP), Internal Family Systems therapy (IFS), and psychedelic psychotherapy, or skills like trauma-memory rewriting or group reenactments that allow us to help our nervous systems get acclimated to the present and correct what should have been corrected a long time ago. Sometimes when we are processing, we have to dig into our skills and resources developed in phase one, and the sense of needing safety happens concurrently with phase two. As we process, the grief comes as we really realize what we went through.

Hear this clearly: when working through trauma, grief is part of healing. Grief *is* the healing. It doesn't feel that way; we often can't fathom that pain is part of ourselves being restored. But grief is not violence or powerlessness of victimization. When we are healing from trauma, grief is seeing what happened with clear eyes and responding to ourselves the way we deserved to be witnessed all along.

Herman's third stage of healing is *reconnection and restoration*, a reintegration of the self that was lost due to trauma and a reintegration of the trauma into the narrative of our self. This means that we have in some ways come to terms with the trauma, and we can look forward, ask what is next, and envision a future outside what happened. We can do this when we feel safe enough in the present to look back on what happened and see it is over. Then the future can begin to appear. This, again, is a form of reconnection. This reconnection is meant to extend beyond us to reconnection with others. It may even mean allowing what happened to us to incite a kind of meaning or purpose that propels us into the world. I imagine this is why so many people who have been hurt by a particular issue decide to mentor others facing that same challenge, become a therapist working with that population, or donate money to that cause.

Although these three phases are sequential, they may feel otherwise. We might expect safety to come at the end, after all the trauma process work. Or we might expect the processing to be the thing we do first. It can also seem confusing that the reconnection and restoration happen at the end. I remember learning about these stages before having done my own work with this model and thinking, *Why would I want to reintegrate? Doesn't that mean I'm getting closer to what I'm trying to get away from?* It is the safety that allows us to face what was otherwise impossible to bear, and this allows us to really have the sense that we survived in a way that allows us to turn toward the awfulness again. In a way, these phases are more like three circles overlapping in a Venn diagram or like phases of the moon—happening over and over again.

The Beginning of a Conversation

There are as many paths to recovering from spiritual trauma as there are people who are recovering. There is no panacea for all the pain, no one goal, no objective measure that healing has happened. The more we can allow for each person to be different—and need different things—the more we can create systems in which healing can take place. Perhaps surprisingly, allowing for different needs, speeds, and routes for healing allows for more connection to take place.

Within that variability, common themes do emerge over and over in the literature on healing. Think of this as an un-finished sentence, a series of experiments, or the beginning of a conversation to be had. In the therapeutic process, we look for what works without being too overwhelming.

You may need to let yourself admit that trauma has happened, or allow someone else to name that for you.

You may find relief in giving yourself the space to tend to the wounds. This can happen a number of ways. You may need to tell the story, or come to realize your body has been telling the story all along—in the form of emotion, poor digestion, tightness in your chest, or fatigue or numbness or anxiety. You may need to learn that other people, even those who are qualified to help you, do not have the right to your vulnerability without earning it.

You may need to get away from a specific spiritual community or leader or gatherings all together. Or you may need to dig deeper into your spiritual communities, traditions, or practices to anchor you, separating them from the behavior of the person or people who hurt you.

You may need to find other forms of relationship that feel therapeutic and noncoercive—with people who know how to care for you—like individual therapy or group therapy or community support.

You may need to make space to grieve the losses. There are so many losses, measurable and immeasurable, existential and relational. You may yearn for time that was lost or years when you could have felt differently. This may mean realizing that relationships that were healthy and loving were dropped, or careers and passions you could have pursued were left to wither. You may grieve your sexuality, your relationship with your body, or other aspects of yourself that were lost because of the system, relationship, or person.

You may also grieve what you lose in giving up on a relationship, faith, or community that caused you harm. You may grieve the lost sense of certainty, a clear plan for your life, defined boundaries around behavior, and feeling of meaning that was beautifully packaged and handed to you. You may grieve the loss of culture and feel the loneliness of its absence. You may experience the strange bottom-dropping-out-from-under-you feeling that comes from realizing that something can feel good and still not be good for you.

If you have been driven to overwork and self-sacrifice to the detriment of your own health and well-being, you may need to take time to receive care and explore all the reactions you have to that. You may need to renegotiate your relationship with finances if financial abuse was part of the trauma for you.

You may need to repair bonds you severed or neglected, tending to the relationships that withered or were disconnected because of what the community or practices demanded of you. This might mean learning how to build relationships with folks who are not part of your faith community or don't share a similar past. You may need to create clear boundaries and determine the kind of experiences and patterns of relationship that are not healthy for you, at least now.

You may need to start feeling your feelings, noticing your body, and paying attention to the stories you tell about your body. You may need to realize that feeling feelings is hard and not an intellectual process. Feeling feelings requires you to trust yourself, and that may be more than you know how to do on your own. You may need to work on tolerating discomfort and distress—especially if you were used to spiritual bypassing or if you were told that any discomfort was the voice of the Spirit telling you something wasn't right.

You may need to realize that the thing you think is trauma sits on top of all sorts of other traumas in your life or in your family or in the systems you are in, which is why it was so hard to see it as trauma in the first place. You may need to work backward to connect with a younger part of yourself.

You may need to learn about the nervous system and how our bodies learn, remember, and process feelings. You likely need to read about emotional regulation and dysregulation, and explore healthy patterns of relationship and power. You may need to research codependency, attachment styles, and consent. You may need to realize that access to information was kept from you and accept that there is so much to learn.

You may need to explore creativity and self-expression. In systems that discourage you from having a self, it can be a slow and sometimes terrifying process to learn to pay attention to what is inside—the impulses, the longings, the life-force energy that moves through our bodies—and follow it. If you have been told this is bad and dangerous, it may take time to learn how to trust that what is inside and yearns to be expressed connects you to more of yourself, makes more of you in the world, and helps you feel the goodness of being alive.

You may need to discover you are good, have always been good, and are deserving of love. You may need to spend time unlearning the stories you were told and setting down the belief that you are unacceptable or fundamentally bad. You may need to be compassionate with how long this takes, and you may need lots of reminders around you in the form of practices and people and stories that help you remember that to be true.

You may need to relearn, or learn for the first time, that this life is yours. This body is yours. Your choices are yours. Being responsible for yourself is an honor, because caring for you and loving you, even when it is you loving and caring for you, are sacred work.

You may need to build new or different belief structures—with new rituals, symbols, or co-journeyers.

And one day, just maybe, you may find a way to make meaning of it all. Even if that meaning is different from how someone else would make meaning. Even if that meaning is that there is no meaning. Even if that simply allows you to say,

"Life is full of pain, and beauty, and here I am in the midst of it."

Religious Residue

In chapter 6, you read about parts inside you and the idea that there are multiple voices, or selves, or behavioral networks that exist inside your nervous system. This helps us understand why sometimes we feel strong and fearless and other times like a child in time-out. Or why one part of us loves to learn and another part of us feels like it needs to be perfect.

When we experience trauma, there is often a part of us that gets stuck in what happens, almost as if there is a younger self inside us who still lives in the moment—or moments—when the trauma happened. We can easily be confused when we get out of a church or relationship or community group and find that we still feel like the old things we thought, felt, did, or believed are with us now, even if we worked so hard to leave them behind. Even years into our lives following the trauma, we can be surprised by the relics of that past popping into our awareness, even if we worked hard to change how we think. No matter how far we have come, there are still fragments or clusters of ideas and feelings floating around inside us.

In working with people who have survived religious trauma, I have learned how often this happens and how alone and ashamed people can feel about it. They feel like they might be the only ones facing the inner conflict of this cognitive and moral dissonance, not realizing that this is a relatively common phenomenon for people who have left or "de-identified" from a religious background. Scholars like Daryl van Tongeren, Nathan DeWall, and their colleagues have called this "religious residue," and they found that individuals who were raised with specific beliefs, attitudes, and behaviors still exhibit the imprint of the religion in these ways, even if they have made great effort to distance themselves from an identity and set of practices associated with their hurt.[1] This can include anything from spending habits to behavior that is caring and generous toward others. Put incisively, Preston Hill says, "Religion is sticky."[2]

The hypothesis that accompanies the research is that this is because of *schema theory*: religion is sticky because it shapes the way we see the world and forms our identity. Although schemas are generally challenging to change, van Tongeren and DeWall highlight how much stickier the schema is when the worldview, thoughts, and identity are thought of as eternal. Habits also play a role, and spiritual or religious practices are usually internalized through repetition. When we learn things, especially over a long period of time or early in our lives, they get baked into the structures in our brains responsible for the most automatic thinking and feeling. The more meaningful something is—and in many cases the more afraid we are of being without it—the more deeply we attach to it.

The residue living inside us from beliefs and practices associated with harm can be extraordinarily painful, at times making it difficult for people to feel like they can fully extricate themselves from the systems that harmed them. They are like echoes following them around wherever they go. For example, we may have learned growing up that people who follow religions different from our own are dangerous and need to be feared. Even after having done so much work to detangle that belief, and as much as our adult self believes otherwise, we might still find we think defensively when interacting with a person from another religion. This can get complicated if we grow up and come to embrace the religion we used to fear. We can both want to be in this religion and sometimes have thoughts that are confusing and archaic related to it. We might feel like a fraud or at war within ourselves.

In the example I just used, you could replace the word *religion* with so many other things: sexual orientation, gender, race, body size, culture, and so on.

It is also possible there is a part inside us that hates where we came from and is embarrassed and ashamed to have been a part of a community or faith or relationship that hurt us so much.

There might also be a part inside us that holds all this unprocessed pain. I imagine this part to be like a bag we hold behind our backs. We funnel painful experiences and memories into it so we don't have to feel them, but it remains there, this bag of pain. And when it starts to overflow, our strategies to manage the pain have to get more blunt and controlling to keep it at bay.

Or there may be a part of us that carries the stories, behaviors, ways of coping, strategies, and beliefs of the person or system that was abusive. This is more common than we may like to admit, but it is so helpful to be aware of and talk about it so we don't go back to that old story of saying "we're bad" without understanding why this is happening. We are so good at learning and adapting and finding ways to stay safe that often when people who are powerful or important to us hurt us, we learn to map their minds, map their behaviors, and anticipate what they will do next. To learn to do this is to anticipate the ways we might get hurt and so not be taken by surprise—to try not to be so hurt by seeing it coming. And a part of us can still carry the memories of what would happen, what would be said, and how to minimize the damage long after we are out of the system.

Sometimes we know we are meeting a story or voice we internalized from someone in the past because we think a thought that feels abusive—almost like it's something that someone would say to someone else—and if we trace it back, we realize that the thought we had sounds a lot like that old leader or the thing our parent used to say. It was never our thought but rather a thing that someone else said to us in such a hurtful way or so frequently that we internalized it, like a recording of their voice in our heads trying to control us. Sometimes the recording is directed at us, but sometimes it is directed at others. And we say or think things about others in this same internalized way.

Add to this list any other part of us that is painful, confusing, and seems out of place in our current life or who we want to be as a grounded, wise adult. These parts of us might seem really different from each other, but the good news is that we actually want to respond to them the same way. Whether it's shame or despair or embarrassment or unprocessed pain, these parts of us developed for a reason and are communicating something important about who we are. Although it might seem confusing to imagine at first, given how much we might want to get rid of the part of us that abuses us or hates our past, even that part has something of value to offer us now if we can be in relationship with it in a healthy way.

Maybe soon or maybe in the very distant future, or maybe never at all, there may come a point where we will choose to look back and see how the people we knew or the practices we engaged in or the times of our lives that seem riddled with grief also offered us experiences that were resources. They might be difficult to see at first, tucked away behind the red flags and open wounds, but there might be parts of us that lovingly hold memories of the kind auntie who always looked us in the eye and made us feel loved, or the friend who really understood, or the feeling of singing in a group, or what it was like to have predictability when everything else felt chaotic, or the lessons of caring for our neighbor. There is no need to tell a story about something being good that was not good. We do not need to do to ourselves what was done to us by others, hiding the pain in service of keeping an image together. However, there is value in meeting with all the parts of you inside, including the parts of you who miss and long for what you once had that felt so good.

If black-and-white thinking is a residue of our spiritual trauma, then learning to see the complexity in our stories can be a part of what allows us to navigate away from the systems and beliefs that were wounding and toward a more integrated view of self and the world. Healing often asks us to do something different from what happened before. While in the past you may have believed you had to banish some emotion, the invitation here is to explore and build a relationship with it. If in the past you tried to pray away your anxiety or fear, I'm suggesting your fear and anxiety are like mini versions of you that deserve to be known and loved. If in the past you felt immense shame for compulsive masturbation, I'm suggesting here that you imagine there is a person who lives inside you who feels this need and instead of shaming them you get to know them and get curious about what they are trying to say—or help you feel or not feel. If there is a part of you that hates your past, try joining with it and chiming in. You remain the wise adult self who feels curiosity, kindness, and compassion to help you be in dialogue with these parts.

To do this, I imagine having tea with a part of myself. Sometimes, if I'm really struggling to engage, I actually pour two cups of tea and sit down across from another chair. I dig deep and find the self inside who is curious, steady, loving, and gentle. Then I start by greeting the part of myself I want to engage and asking it some questions. If this way doesn't work, I write down my thoughts in the form of a dialogue. It helps to remember that no matter what this part of me is saying, it is always from the past or is a younger version of me. I find it really helpful to listen and look for the good intentions of whatever emotional part of myself I'm with. How is that part trying to help me?

Even the part of you that hates your past, hates who you were and where you come from, is trying to help you. If I had to guess, I would say that the hate toward yourself is the hate or abuse around you that you learned to internalize to blend in or survive. This emotion can also be there trying to push away the memories of what was and give you distance from it so you can heal. In other words, the hate you feel is trying to help you be different, because you really want to be different.

After verifying your positive intention, thank the part of you that you are with, ask it to tell its story and what support it would need to heal, and give it validation. I often like to do this by letting the part know that it is so valuable and I really appreciate its efforts to protect me, which I really needed when I was unsafe or hurt. But now I'm in the present. I'm safe and I know who I am and what is true, and so I don't need it to keep protecting me. I often remind the part that I am the age I am and give it the story of how I got here—just in case that part of me isn't quite sure that I really did grow up and get away from that situation. We can do this even if the situation we feel stuck in is from a year ago or last week. We are always growing up, learning more, gaining insight, and moving forward.

If you're not sure what to say, you could imagine someone you love and trust sitting across from this part of you. Imagine them saying to this part of you:

I believe you matter.

I believe you are important and have something to say worth listening to.

I believe that when you are heard, we can work together so you don't have to work harder than you need to, and I can appreciate you for all the ways you kept me safe so long ago.

Sometimes giving up on what we once knew, as familiar and right as we thought it was, is part of the cycle of growth and rebirth. Sometimes the thing we need to lose or set down is not the story of our past or who we actually are but how we learned to get away from what is inside us. Or in my adaptation of the words of a first-century Jewish mystic, when we set down what we had to believe in order to survive, what felt like our entire lives, that is when we begin to find ourselves again.[3]

The Power of Knowledge

I have learned from working with others and from my own healing journey that digging into research can help us heal from spiritual trauma. Rigorous, peer-reviewed data can lend some certainty, clarity, and sense-making when so much has been flipped upside down or when a lack of information or misinformation has been one of the ways we have been injured or kept from agency. To be sure, it can be tempting to switch one authority for another, but there can be power, healing, and humanity in the right kind of information—delivered the right kind of way. So with that in mind, here are some research findings about healing from spiritual trauma that I want to highlight for you.

The Challenges of Leaving Religion

In 2018, Craig Cashwell and Paula Swindle published an article called "When Religion Hurts: Supervising Cases of

Religious Abuse."[4] They begin by stating that research has shown that spirituality and religion can be resources for people experiencing trauma, but religious and spiritual practices and communities can also contribute to client problems or worsen symptoms of mental health issues. They highlight the tension of recognizing that something religious or spiritual is implicated in the traumatic experience while also holding that spirituality can be a powerful resource for healing from trauma. It's important to work through spiritual trauma in ways that honor both the person and their personal experiences and development.

The article goes on to say that there are some specific tasks to healing trauma in a therapeutic setting: owning the experiences as abusive and traumatizing, coming to terms with how those experiences impact one's belief system, making space to grieve the losses, and building a new community—especially when a previous community has been lost. This article reminded me that, for some, leaving a religious community that was traumatic might be a marker of a certain kind of power, stability, or social support that exists outside of the religious community. If one's whole world is tied up in a community and culture and years of family tradition, then leaving might be impossible or at least a catastrophic loss. For others who have varied social connections, leaving a specific community after trauma might feel like a relief with immediate benefits.

The authors go on to say that those who have experienced spiritual trauma might be more likely to struggle with articulating that the experience was abuse or trauma, they might struggle to hold others accountable, and they might find it difficult to explore the impact this has had on their beliefs and spirituality moving forward. For some, the perception that they are speaking ill of their church or their religion might come with profound guilt and fear, making it difficult for them to categorically define the experience in such a way that would support them in processing the impact. Some may be forced out of their religious community, which can compound the loss due to feelings of shame and rejection.

The authors highlight how central power dynamics are in the process of religious and spiritual trauma. When God is thought to have orchestrated the traumatic experience, it can create a profound sense of powerlessness that extends beyond the context within which the event occurred. If God is responsible and God is everywhere, then there is nowhere they are safe. It can be helpful to recognize how patterns of abusive power may show up in a person's life in multiple ways or numerous relationships.

Therapists working with spiritual trauma need to be comfortable talking about spirituality. Whatever their own background may be, they need to understand the varied ways spirituality and religion can be connected to mental health presentations—perhaps helpful in some cases, neutral in others, and in still other cases can create trauma or exacerbate mental health conditions. Therapists must be able to attend to how their own biases and beliefs shape their clinical work. It is my hope that no client would attend therapy to process spiritual trauma and, after describing how prayer was used as a manipulative tool for clergy abuse, would have a therapist who then tried to include prayer in the session. It is also my hope that no client would show up to therapy wanting to work on spiritual trauma and the therapist assumes it means they no longer hold dear their theological convictions or spiritual practices. In both cases, whether it's spiritual bypassing or the therapist's own reactions, this is misattuned, and effective therapy is attuned therapy.

Healing and Growth Following Trauma

The second article was published in 2013 by Rosemary de Castella and Janette Graetz Simmonds and outlines the findings from research interviews with individuals who experienced religious and spiritual growth after traumatic experiences.[5] Previous research on post-traumatic growth had found that some people experience positive outcomes after something traumatic happens. After trauma, some people develop new understandings of themselves or the world, and they begin to think about the future differently and how they can live life with purpose or direction. Further research found that this post-traumatic growth was tied to spirituality and religion and that for some people religion and spirituality can play a role in predicting if post-traumatic growth will occur.

As we've discussed, spirituality is, among other things, the inborn desire and search for meaning, interconnection, and what is sacred. And trauma is, among other things, a wound to the spiritual that shatters our assumptions about the world and connection. But in this study of survivors of various forms of trauma, de Castella and Simmonds found that one year after the traumas, post-traumatic growth had occurred for these individuals and that it was deeply connected to their spirituality. This finding is hopeful in that it suggests that our instinct to search, yearn, and connect remains intact and accessible. This supports post-trauma healing that goes beyond the management of anxiety and stress and memories into the kind of well-being that we would all hope for on the other side of something awful.

The authors identified that for participants who experienced post-traumatic spiritual and religious growth, the spirituality they experienced before the trauma was central. Following the trauma, they experienced an inner yearning and desire for connection. They understood their challenges as part of their spiritual growth and sought to find meaning in their suffering. They experienced sacredness in the here and now and found that, following trauma, their sense of spirituality deepened and the formality of their religious beliefs changed or softened. Not surprisingly, the participants in the study had a fundamental shift in their worldview. They found themselves rediscovering who they were following trauma. This included choosing new likes and interests and friends as well as learning to see themselves as strong for what they had lived through. They experienced a change in their values that prioritized honor, vulnerability, and relationships over achievement and material gain. Consistent with what we have already discussed, a sense of social connection and support was intimately connected to the experience of spiritual and religious growth following trauma.

To be clear, the article didn't cover people for whom spirituality or religion was a central feature in the trauma. And—as is the case with all qualitative research—we can't generalize from it to all people or suggest that a person not in the study should behave or think like the participants. Even still, reading it had me thinking of the benefits that come from widening our knowledge base. We can learn things about ourselves as we process trauma and talk about what happened. This can help us make informed decisions about what matters to us and who we want to be moving forward. The scientific literature shows us that we are always capable of learning, growing, and changing our minds right up until the moment we die. Trauma, no matter how devastating, early, or long-lasting, can never take that away from us. Even in its devastating blow to our spirit, the trauma is not more powerful than the drive inside us to survive. I hold that truth close to me and hold the hope of it for others. I believe it's possible to do that without minimizing the devastation of the wounding or assuming this is how others will or should feel.

For some, the conversation about post-traumatic growth needs to be off the table. You are welcome to have a reaction that I'm even bringing up post-traumatic growth, and you can thank your reaction as a marker of self-protection not to rush you or anyone else out of the pain you are allowed to feel for as long as it takes. But for those of you who might see some possibility here and feel a tug inside you, I am curious to know what it could mean for you to know that healing and growth can be found on the other side of trauma.

When we have experienced the rigid and controlling beliefs that often go along with spiritual trauma, sometimes just the thought of a changing faith can feel dangerous, shameful, or like a kind of loss. We might have been led to believe that an abandonment of some kind of belief can only be negative, instead of seeing it as a possibility for the kind of growth we have been craving, praying for, and hoping for all along. Leaving behind the beliefs and values that hurt us so deeply can be a mark of growth. Separating what was untrue and hurtful from what remains true, without shaming ourselves for not having previously seen the difference, can also be a mark of growth. Depending on where you are and what language you like to use, perhaps it is the hand of God that holds people close and walks them away from certain beliefs that do not reflect the true nature of God.

Healing the Shame Imparted by Purity Culture

In her study of healing from sexual shame, Kelsey Siemens researched adult women immersed in the Christian purity movement of the 1990s who found a way to move past shame in constructive and embodied ways.[6] Growing up within purity culture, these women were taught that complying with rigid sexual ideals was intimately tied to their spirituality, moral goodness, sexual safety, social belonging, and desirability. They were also taught that as women they were responsible for men's actions (even in the cases of assault and abuse), that their value as a woman would be diminished if they experienced sexuality outside of heterosexual marriage, and that their (sexual) bodies were bad. This led to experiences of profound sexual shame, disembodiment, and isolation. This shame became the lens through which they viewed their bodies and sexuality, contributing to decreased arousal, desire, sexual engagement, and pleasure. Additionally, it manifested as confusion, physical discomfort, psychological and bodily numbing, fragmented self-image, body hatred, and disconnection in relationships with others and themselves.

In spite of the purity culture messaging that suppressed their sexuality and connection to their bodies, these women were motivated to work through the shame and came to know freedom, intimacy, and sexual embodiment—fully experiencing their sexuality through their entire selves. This process enabled them to access agency and power within their bodies and remain connected to their needs, desires, and pleasure within relationships.

Siemens's findings about how this healing process happens are fascinating, offering clues about the pathway forward for healing sexual shame as well as the other forms of body shame or mind/body fragmentation pervasive for those with spiritual trauma. To heal, these women engaged in deliberate steps, individually and relationally, including seeking out information about their bodies and sexuality, learning how to attune to their bodies, going to therapy, and thinking critically about the messages they received that had hurt them. Naming and processing their purity culture and sexual shame experiences was essential; it was a liberation from the silence about sexuality imposed on them by their community and an opportunity to connect with others in a way that offered healing from feelings of shame and isolation.

These women were able to reflect on the messages they had heard about sexuality and push back and to internalize new messages that better aligned with their values and what they wanted to believe about sexuality, relationships, and their identity more broadly. In contrast to the silence and control about sexuality they experienced growing up, they discussed their sexuality with friends and partners in ways that were honest, open, and ultimately healing, noting how friendship with other supportive and critically thinking women was a primary source of their resilience. Through experiencing authentic, empathetic healing encounters with others and having embodied, positive, and transcendent sexual experiences, these women deepened and integrated their understanding that sex is good and can even be a potential pathway to the sacred.

The Role of Attachment in Healing from Spiritual Trauma

The last article I want to share was published in 2013 by Alyson Stone.[7] Stone starts by highlighting how few resources there are for those who experience spiritual wounds because religion and spirituality are most often understood as sources of meaning, connection, and strength—even in academic literature. While that is true for many, a lack of resources has left clinicians, and those experiencing spiritual trauma, without good, evidence-based interventions. She highlights the work of Donald Winnicott (an important voice in the psychology world when it comes to attachment and child development) and discusses the harm of having to develop a kind of false self to meet the expectations of family and society.[8] Rigid religious belief systems result in people having to develop a false self slowly over time to fit into categories of what is acceptable. Previous research has found that people with spiritual trauma rarely seek therapy and that the effects linger unaddressed. These wounds are often uncovered as slowly as they developed: within the context of a relationship or relationships where there is psychological freedom to say or think or feel whatever needs to be said or thought or felt and without fear of judgment or punishment.

Stone notes that attachment is central for the process of healing. For many people, their relationship with God was an attachment relationship. She highlights previous research that recognizes that attachment with God can be like attachment relationships we have with parents or partners. They can be secure and stable or anxious, dismissive, and avoidant. Even once a person has left a religious or spiritual environment that was abusive, or has changed their beliefs or practices, these deeply held patterns of relating to God and others can still linger. Thankfully, these internal maps for connection and relating can change.

Communities and Contexts That Help Us Flourish

Understanding trauma disrupts us in a way that is useful and healthy. It seems to defy the ideas that make us think of ourselves in the fragmented ways we have in the past. We are enabled to see each individual as a system of mind and body and brain and inner being. We are reminded of our interconnection with other systems and our place in the larger networks of life around us. The more I work with and understand trauma, the less I believe that it is an individual phenomenon. Our perception of it being about individuals—just minds, just bodies, just this person or that person—is itself a symptom of the trauma.

There is no way to talk about trauma and the people who experience it without talking about the context within which it emerges, and the even wider circles of influence. There are things we can intentionally do to create systems that are less likely to create harm. I believe that even though we are good at our core, we will still sometimes hurt each other, misunderstand one another, and make choices or act in ways that make it hard for others to flourish. When we know how to repair those relational wounds and take responsibility for them, we can create communities where people can flourish. It is especially important for leaders in spiritual communities to be aware of the influence they carry and to accept responsibility for creating safe spaces within which people can heal, grow, and flourish.

A healthy spiritual community will do the following:

- Prioritize the psychological health of community members rather than fostering the impression that people must follow prescribed behaviors as a condition of belonging. This means encouraging members to have boundaries, allowing them to make choices about how much or in what way they participate, and honoring their autonomy. It also means people aren't shamed or belittled if they decide to leave and that community members are encouraged to connect with those outside the community.

- Create space for diverse viewpoints by maintaining thoughtful dialogue, mutual care, and respect for others' choices. This requires a community to learn how to tolerate emotions, experience them, and regulate them. Respect for others also requires building a community in which people are supported to respect and care for themselves. Critical thought and the use of reason in coming to conclusions or making choices are needed.

- Have support and care for leaders that allows them to be human but also ensures those leaders have accountability, can receive feedback, and will listen to others. Communities need leaders who can self-reflect on their challenges and limitations and work with others who have giftings they do not, instead of assuming they can do it all themselves. Leaders aren't exempt from the same standards of behavior that all other members of the community must follow. Leaders are allowed and deserving of the same kind of care as everyone else in the community. No one is expected to have unquestioning loyalty to the leader. No leader should be expected to be perfect or to carry the demands of an entire community on their shoulders. Leaders deserve to have good mental health care without this implying they are morally or spiritually inferior.

- Strive to love, find connection with, and promote the flourishing of all people. This means not believing they (as individuals or as a group) are more valuable, more special, or more holy than anyone else—both inside the community and outside it.

- Appreciate the complexity of embodied experiences and have awareness of how the spiritual community has been a place of disembodiment and self-fragmentation (and how the roots or foundations of the community have supported disembodiment and self-fragmentation). This means recognizing that we are bodies and that our bodies are worth caring for and honoring. Again, this requires making space for emotions, trauma, disabilities, and movement. It also means becoming aware of the ways that the socially created hierarchy of body ideals has infiltrated faith— including the moralization of body size, disability, race, and gender—and finding ways to disentangle spiritual practices and the community from perpetuating body hierarchies.

- Respect individuals and their right to participate or not participate. No one should be coerced into activities that require significant commitments of time, energy, membership, or money. Some spiritual practices or rituals within religious contexts involve mind/consciousness altering, such as trance states or ecstatic experiences coming from emotionally heighted and extended group worship experiences. These are not necessarily bad, but people need to have choices about whether they participate and should not be punished or rejected for choosing not to or for wanting more information about these practices. In healthy spiritual and religious environments, unrealistic promises for healing, transformation, or supernatural experiences are not made. Regardless of the spiritual community's position on spiritual gifts, using them in a way that respects others is important. This can also include not making assumptions or interpretations about others that you don't have the knowledge or permission to make and then wrapping them in spiritual language about divine insight and words of knowledge.

- Work to make space for the aspects of human experience that are painful without spiritual bypassing. The community should be encouraged to lament, grieve, feel sadness, tell the truth about pain, and experience emotion in the body. Members should not be encouraged to use defenses or reach for superstitions or the prosperity gospel. The community must also allow for doubt, uncertainty, curiosity, and the changing of one's mind.

SAFE Communities

Preston Hill, whom we heard from earlier, recommends practices represented by the acronym SAFE for communities to become trauma-safe.[9] These communities are meant to be supporting for those who have survived trauma, but ultimately they create the conditions under which we all can flourish. He describes the practices this way:

S: Safety First
Hill describes this as a difficult place to start because many communities prioritize spiritual values over the actions needed to make communities safe. Hill says, "If you give me the option between humans flourishing and being safe, or some other spiritual value, and you're saying that the other one is better, to me that is gaslighting 101."

A: Active Listening
The second point refers to the role of the community in being open to the stories of trauma survivors. Sometimes listening to and honoring trauma survivors can seem threatening to spiritual communities, but hearing what survivors have to say not only creates the conditions under which they can experience more healing but also transforms those who are listening.

As David Augsburger said, "Being listened to is so close to being loved that most people cannot tell the difference."[10]

F: Fostering Agency

Agency is an essential ingredient for communities to be a welcome place for survivors, to decrease the risk of becoming abusive, and to create spaces to heal. Hill describes this as being empowered and given control over how much or little to disclose. A person's self-knowing is honored, respected, and fostered.

E: Engaging the Body

Embodiment is ultimately about creating space for autonomy. Although this promotes healing and the developing of a healthy and robust sense of self, Hill highlights how this inoculates people against gaslighting. Hill notes that paying attention to our bodies fosters spiritual and moral discernment and allows us to assess our environment. This can lead us to ask questions about dynamics at play, how they impact us, and what they remind us of that might have hurt us. Listening to the wisdom of our bodies helps us sense what is right for us.

You might remember from chapter 3 that processes of abuse and trauma can be replicated in multiple layers of overlapping systems, the small systems reflecting dynamics of harm occurring within the larger systems. This is also true of healing: what is healing on a large scale can mirror what happens at an individual level.

SAFE is useful both for creating trauma-safe spiritual communities in which individuals are supported to heal and thrive and for guiding the individual or smaller systems toward health.

Safety, listening, agency, and embodiment are key building blocks of human development. We could view this as a kind of hierarchy of needs, where safety begets attuned and responsive connecting, followed by the development of agency, and this gives way to the experience of being fully embodied in the world—through which we experience support for our expression, protection, and intuition. As a result, I can imagine a person using SAFE as a framework for organizing their way of relating to themselves, creating a foundation of skills or principles that support flourishing and trauma recovery in intimate partnerships, or even evaluating which therapist to work with.

◆ ◆ ◆

As I think about the process of healing, I am reminded of how often the journey can feel unpredictable, winding, and disorganized. We can feel anxious for the distress to be over and might ask, "How long will this take?" But just as trauma and the effects of it are nonlinear, not relegated to a singular moment of time, so is healing. Sometimes when we begin to see and turn toward the injuries, even though this can be painful, this is when the healing begins to take place. The time we thought was fine was actually when the wounding was taking place; when we realized it was not fine, that was when we began to mend. Sometimes we think we are either recovered or recovering, and others do too, and we are really just beginning. And sometimes it is when we can look at the places of wounding, really look, without turning away, that there is proof of more healing than we may realize. The process of labeling and seeing the trauma is actually—if we look closely enough—an act of healing, especially when we do this as systems and communities. Bearing witness to the trauma, coming close enough to listen, imagining the pain of those who are hurting, and acknowledging our own pain tell us that something new is beginning to grow.

Because he often says things better than I ever could, let me offer the words of Rainer Maria Rilke: "Be patient toward all that is unsolved in your heart and try to love the questions themselves, like locked rooms and like books that are now written in a very foreign tongue. Do not now seek the answers, which cannot be given you because you would not be able to live them. And the point is, to live everything. Live the questions now. Perhaps you will then gradually, without noticing it, live along some distant day into the answer."[11]

If you are on the journey of healing, I want you to know that I have hope that things will get better. I have seen enough people heal from unimaginable traumas that I have hope, limitless and unshakable hope, that you too can recover and that something new can grow in the space occupied by the injury. You can peel back the layers of stories you have carried like loads on your back and find again under it all what was always true of you before you ever learned otherwise. If you find it hard to hope, you can borrow mine. Or know that I'm carrying yours for you until you can carry it yourself.

⬩ PRACTICE ⬩
Embodied Agency

Disruptions to agency are characteristic of traumatic experiences and systems, meaning that finding ways to rehearse and restore our sense of choice, control, and the power to act on our lives can be central to our ability to show our nervous systems the trauma is over and we are here now. Even if these practices seem small, our ability to have choice and power over our own bodies and to act on that in the present moment is cumulative. We can accumulate and store the impact of the experience in our bodily memory of ourselves for the more challenging moments when we most need to have agency. You might try this exercise in this moment even if you feel relatively safe and calm, keeping in mind that we have a much better chance of internalizing a new skill if we practice it over and over again in low-stakes situations. As you practice over time, the opportunity for choice and agentic action will become more available in your awareness in moments when you might feel overwhelmed, powerless, or stuck.

These practices often start with settling yourself, taking some breaths, or adjusting your posture. But for the sake of this exercise, I want to invite you to notice how you are feeling right now, even before you make any adjustments. What is a choice you can make in this moment to support yourself as a body? Pay attention to posture, temperature, thirst, or even the desire for stillness or movement. Having done that, or in the process of doing that, you might say to yourself, "I have the ability to notice how I feel and make choices about how to better support myself as a body." Before we go further, if any of these suggestions do not feel right for you, I invite you to notice where the "no" lives in your body and whether it feels good to you. I invite you to say "no" out loud or in your head to the sentence prompt.

When you are ready, you might consider making a choice about how you are as a body, any choice at all, simply for the purpose of flexing your control muscle. Think about what might be tolerable for you: slowing down your breathing, finding a relaxed position, putting this book down and doing some stretches, whatever you like. Notice how it feels to have made that choice simply because you could. After doing so, you might think about how you want to express yourself in this moment, first thinking about what is inside you (what feelings, senses, impulses, images, colors, patterns of movement, etc.). As you connect with this sensation, try putting it into expression (perhaps using movement, sound, or words or by making something with your hands).

You might notice how it felt to do this exercise.

Roberto Che Espinoza on Communal Healing and Belonging

I want to introduce you to Roberto Che Espinoza. Roberto is special to me as a friend. My personal life is richer because they are in it, but they also have a public voice that I continue to learn from, particularly as they speak to the various layers of Bronfenbrenner's systems that shape our development. As a neurodivergent, nonbinary, transguy, a Latinx public theologian and philosopher who is also ordained as a Baptist minister, Roberto, through his life and work, keeps calling us back to more of ourselves, toward community, embodiment, justice, and our collective healing, and telling the truth about the legacies of the systems we live in. If Roberto has something to say, I want to listen to it. So when they agreed to talk to me about spiritual trauma and the healing journey, I knew they would share a perspective I didn't want to go without.

Roberto

The call for holistic healing is not just for our individual body but also for our collective body, our communal body, our cultural body. And when we take that seriously, when we take the quality of connection with attaching ourselves to ourselves or remembering ourselves, that's how we heal. And it's iterative, it's tedious, it's an everyday practice. Every morning I wake up in a body that I don't know, and I sit on the edge of the bed and I place my bare feet on the carpet and I press my feet into the ground and I imagine roots going into the ground. And that's how I am healing. Along with therapy every week and spiritual direction every month and medicine every day.

It takes a diversity of tactics.

[After leaving a harmful community,] it was incumbent on me to figure out what was next. I didn't think about returning to a White, privileged, affluent community. I just didn't think they were my people. And now people reach out to me all the time: Are you pastoring anywhere? Are you convening people? And always my answer is no. But the best times that I've had that feel like religious experiences are when my table is full: Where the food is flowing. Where there is no hierarchy. Where there's quality of connection happening. Where there is abundance in emotional capacity and reflection. And don't get me wrong, the vision of church as I understand it from reading the stories of Jesus is a really great vision. I just think we are deeply compromised and are unable to attain that vision because of capitalism, White supremacy, the war machine, and the ways we have constructed power and our ideology. It gets mixed in there. We don't know how to be human with one another.

That's part of the reason why church doesn't work anymore. We have relied on what I would call a "passive epistemology," where we're being spoon-fed from the pulpit to the pew. And the vision of church was to be this mutually reciprocal community, and community is to be connected in union with one another. And community has compassion. And the Latin root for *compassion* means "suffering with." And we don't know how to do that as people in relationship with ourselves and each other, or in community. I just think that it's bound up in relationships, and I think certainly the Global North and the West are failing at relationships. And we're too tied to things like platform culture, celebrity culture. We expect people with a platform to give us the right dose in a message or in a tweet or an Instagram post. The reliance on that kind of material or information may seem innocuous, but taken to the extreme it's frankly quite dangerous. It separates our self from ourself and each other, and we become reliant on a kind of cult of personality. I've always been very wary of that, which is why I try to be in conversation with those who follow me on social media and actually compost platform culture into community.

I just don't think platforms will save us. I think people can embody a spirituality that is whole and wholesome and healing. I think that those of us who have been harmed by the church or by institutions, or people in leadership or power, even though we may feel bereft of belonging, there is belonging to be had. And it's first becoming curious about ourselves and then each other, and then learning how to suture the attachment wounds that we carry.

EIGHT

Unsettling Ourselves

As I started to work on this book, I asked the people in my life about their experiences of spiritual trauma. You can imagine this was unsettling for some, relieving for others, and more often than not led us to important places. One question connected to one story, followed by another, followed by dropping into a pocket of memories and places that transported them to a life that felt so different from the one they were living now. Days later I would get more texts, there would be more phone calls, and it seemed like there were so many things surfacing, just waiting for a space to be witnessed, memories waiting to be held in the relational spaces where they would be known and honored.

After one of these conversations, a dear friend sent me a message letting me know how relieved she feels to be at the church she attends now. In her weekly community group, no one is forced to pray aloud, no one is expected to orate a prophetic word, and no one has to close their eyes or fold their hands during prayer if they don't want to. She described the relief in her body that came from that space and the freedom to choose.

We talked about how some spiritual communities clearly seem to prefer certain personality types. In some contexts, the person who is silent, perhaps shy or introverted, is praised for being more spiritually mature because of how slow they are to speak. Those who are playful, fast to speak, loud in voice and opinions are identified as immature spiritually or even sinful.

In other contexts or church cultures, the extrovert is considered ideal. They are perceived to be filled with the Spirit, free, jubilant. This temperament, or even the overtalking that can arise from difficulty with being at rest or in silence, is held up as the ideal. And the person who has no capacity or desire to speak aloud in front of others, let alone pray in front of a group, is considered less full of the Spirit, perhaps even needing intervention, correction, or prayer.

As we talked about this, my dear friend explained how she felt shamed and devalued because of her gentle demeanor. When she mentioned the times she felt pressured and manipulated to behave in a way that felt dehumanizing and stressful or she was coerced into an ideal of spirituality, she showed me something I hadn't considered. As a person who more naturally fit into the temperament style expected of me in the communities of faith I was a part of, I experienced the benefits and praise of having a demeanor that was idealized.

All of a sudden I saw myself a little more clearly, remembering the times when I had done to people I loved what had been done to my friend: I had squeezed people into boxes marked "more godly" or "less godly," "more valued" or "less valued," based on some spiritual ideal that had been created by the community I was a part of as an evaluative tool. Then, just as painfully, I began to imagine and remember the times I had caused spiritual harm to others I didn't know. I did or said things at the time because I believed or had been told they were loving things to do or say. They were a way to protect people from the badness of the world or the badness inside them—all things I now was beginning to see differently.

I will never forget this conversation because it opened up something I didn't want to unsee, I couldn't unsee, and raised some questions I needed to ask: How had I caused wounds in others? How had I perpetrated spiritual trauma? What systems had I not only benefited from but also loved that had hurt so many people? What are the legacies of that hurt even to this day? Why did it take me so long to ask these questions? And what do I do about that past now?

I want to pause here to say that I think there is something essential about the need for many of us who are in the church or have a personal or ancestral history with Christianity to look at the wounds that our ancestors and the systems we have been a part of, at least peripherally, have caused. This is especially necessary if we have never done this either individually or collectively, or if we have been telling a story of superiority as a faith community that aligns us most with dominant expressions of power at the cost of others. I am not saying that every Christian community is damaging or dangerous; I actually believe otherwise. Many faith communities have emerged as a form of resistance to dominant systems of power. Such communities have done much to be havens for protecting cultural identity, language, and love for whomever society has decided is "other." However, some communities have not examined their relationship to authoritarian power, settler colonialism, or the people groups they have harmed. Doing so is an important step to being in right relationship with each other; repairing broken relationships with the land, the ancestors we have come from, and the Indigenous communities that are still very much among us; and guiding the work we need to do to build different systems and to mend the wounds of the ones that have caused such destruction in the name of God.

Looking at the legacy of pain that stretches beyond us can be a powerful tool of undoing our aloneness, seeing the systems and processes at play in perpetuating harm, and empowering us to know the ways we can make a difference. In some cases, doing this can assist our own healing by showing us ways we can be involved in making systemic changes, thus protecting others from the same hurt we experienced. Looking at the hurt we've caused requires courage to wade into the pit of grief, knowing we have ground beneath us, a spark inside us, and a community around us that will support us so we won't collapse into a hopeless spiral of shame. So as we venture into this topic and begin asking questions about the spiritual wounds we have caused, I want to invite you to reflect on how this fits into your journey of healing and whether this is something that could propel you into more wholeness or if this is something to come back to later, after the wounds that live inside you get some care before widening your attention to the circles and systems around you.

Staying Connected to Hard Feelings

Moving forward on this topic, it is important to continue tracking our somatic process as we encounter challenging material. You might remember the triangle of experience from chapter 5 and how, when we struggle to stay with core feelings that move us into connection, action, and health, we can easily get caught in our defenses.

There are obvious defenses: denial, avoidance, distraction, judgment, guilt, and stonewalling. Other less obvious defenses include despair, depression, and collapse, or we encounter the inhibitory blocks of anxiety or shame. All of these prevent us from feeling what's hard to feel in our bodies—the sadness and the profound ache of grief that are appropriate when we see hurt and our role in it. The core emotions, you might remember, come in wave form. When we stay with them long enough and let them build until they crest and then settle, we can get to action. Not the kind of action we rush into as a way to avoid the feeling but rather action that is wise, informed by feeling and reflection, and sustainable over time.

So if you do choose to move forward, perhaps you might draw a triangle or hold on to the question "What do I feel in my body?" to remind you to return to your embodied emotional experience, especially as it returns you to the feelings that are essential to move you into healthy action. If disconnecting from our feelings is part of how we bypass, then connecting with our feelings while encountering difficult material is already doing something different. If you are used to thinking your way out of problems, or rationalizing as a way of sense-making, then staying in the senselessness or asking for someone to join you in your not knowing is already a way of doing things differently. Actions like this help us step into more wholeness and connection. And if you find yourself going into shame, I invite you to remember that I too am feeling the sadness and fear and disgust that live underneath and that you are not alone. Imagine joining me in the complexity of staying with all of this.

You might not be surprised to learn that I did a thorough academic search on the psychological theory and research about perpetrating spiritual trauma and the necessary steps to healing. You also might not be surprised to learn that I didn't find much of anything. This is what we call a "paucity of research," because the gaping hole indicates a kind of poverty. Spiritual trauma, as you know, is still happening and will continue to happen. But what are the steps to healing for those who may be perpetuating spiritual trauma, both in their own lives and in their communities?

Because there are so few resources, at least of the kind I can rely on to provide evidence-based intervention, I'm pulling from work about the perpetration of other forms of trauma. But this is complicated, because actions that can result in spiritual trauma exist on a continuum—from the seemingly innocuous comments parents make to their children (they were bad and broken from the start), to the criminal (like clergy sexual abuse), to the systems wide trauma that spans generations (like the oppression and cultural genocide of Indigenous people).

We know that abusive behaviors and systems are motivated by power and control. And power and control are almost always a defense and management system for fear. Sometimes the fear is so buried that a person or a group of people doesn't even know fear is what is motivating them, nor can they see what was at play a long time ago when the pattern of managing the fear originally developed.

From what I have seen and read, individuals who are perpetuating spiritual trauma at high levels of institutional leadership, where it impacts large groups of people, will rarely admit to causing spiritual harm. They likely have institutions around them that endorse them and scaffold their abusive behavior or hide it from plain sight. They also typically have large groups of followers who support their work and don't know that charismatic leadership often masks domination, control, and abuse. These people, if ever held accountable, likely have such profound defenses in place that they wouldn't acknowledge their hurtful behavior or seek support for the pain inside that is causing such harm. Sometimes it can be more productive to help the people around them develop health to ensure the patterns of abuse cannot continue with so much systemic support. These people perpetuating harm often need long-term support, significant losses to help them finally consider the impact of their actions, and robust mental health intervention with consistent, skillful care. Not surprisingly, for many perpetrators of spiritual abuse, mental health supports are taboo, or simply become a box to check, which makes it very difficult for them to access the tender and vulnerable places they need to acknowledge before change is possible.

There's another category of leaders, those who don't have abusive characteristics and legions of supporters scaffolding abuse, but they've been tasked with leading incredibly unhealthy communities while living with the expectation of perfection without access to support. They are crumbling under the pressure and thus acting out in ways that signal distress that feels too hard and deep to name. These leaders often have mountains of their own untended wounds, covered up with coping strategies, and nowhere to turn for self-care.

I have incredible hope for this group of spiritual leaders, especially during the moments when it seems like things are collapsing around them. The facade is found out, the defenses are cracking, and the truth is finally coming out about what has happened behind closed doors. These individuals are frequently able to grasp the impact of their actions and why they drifted so far from themselves in an effort to manage their inner worlds. I have worked with and seen up close the psychological struggle and complexity for these leaders who are forced, in public, to look at what they have done and the damage it has caused. They are able to see that there are consequences that must be faced and can be motivated to tend to their own wounds and begin to address the root causes.

If this is you, I want you to know, if not now, then at some point, that I imagine you to have been riding the incredibly thin edge of profound despair but now to be on the precipice of something new. I believe there is a you inside who has the fortitude to tolerate the impact of what you have done and turn toward the parts inside you that caused this pain, all while believing that you too are deserving of care. I want to stand on that edge with you, or imagine going back in time to the moments you felt this way, and remind you that the kind of leaders our world needs are the ones who look inward, take responsibility for the damage they have done, and invite in healthier systems and patterns—even in cases where this might mean stepping aside all together.

Then I think of the rest of us, those who did exactly what we were told, tried to be good in the eyes of our community, and out of a dangerous mix of fear, love, and unexamined conviction stepped into the role of trying to rescue, save, or heal others without knowing how these efforts might instead inflict harm.

I think of the youth leaders who told kids that girls' sexuality was a threat to boys' morality.

I think of the leaders who suggested the child with Down syndrome could be healed through prayer, rituals, or recipes.

I think of the White Westerners who went on mission trips to build houses and evangelize, believing they had the right way of thinking and behaving that others needed to adopt, never acknowledging the lasting damage this caused to the culture and community after they left.

I think of the parent who disciplined their child with a paddle because someone told them it was the best way to love them.

I think of community members who arranged to send the gay teen to conversion therapy because they thought things would be better if the attraction went away.

I think of the people who pressured their friend to forgive an abuser, believing doing so would help the friend find freedom.

I think of the people who stood outside abortion clinics and hospitals, believing that shaming women and shouting people down were ways to be for life.

I think of the biblical counselors who told people with mental illness to pray more or memorize more Scripture.

I think of the administrators who told women they couldn't speak from a position of authority because they thought this was a way to protect the women from their own sin and suffering.

I think of every woman who told another woman how to behave within a group—to be more desirable—all to help the woman be chosen by a man she thought would make her feel valuable.

I think of every church that believed that conquering the ends of the earth was a way to love, that thought that giving people the Word of God in the form of White culture and colonization was a way to save them from eternal suffering.

I think of every church, churchgoer, leader, staff member, missionary, evangelist, preacher, and pastor so convinced of their exceptionalism or superiority that the thought never occurred to them to look at where that belief came from and who it was hurting.

Healing, Justice, and the Road Forward

When I think about healing, justice, and the road forward, the incredible complexity and variability of each situation stare back at me. There are so many situations requiring their own attuned responses that I couldn't presume to offer a one-size-fits-all prescription to make things better. Yet there are three categories for steps forward I want to share with you that do more than just "fix." Rather, they touch on the places of injury that are likely familiar to all of us in some way. People who hope for healing and restored justice will (1) remain open to feeling pain, (2) stay curious, and (3) seek to repair.

Remain Open to Feeling Pain

First, we need to let ourselves feel the pain that comes from knowing that, in spite of our good intentions, we have hurt other people. This can feel agonizing but becomes easier if we can avoid veering into shutdown, despair, and shame. Grief isn't meant to be something we shoulder alone but rather something we hold in process in community with others, with the safety to explore what happened and why without separating us from one another.

Being able to tolerate our own feelings, without rushing to defend our actions or trying to fix the pain we caused in others, helps us find space for other people to be witnessed. Avoiding this pain can prompt us to jump in, making the process of what comes next all about us—to show people how sorry we are and desperate to rush the process along. Instead, we need to slow down to be with a grief that deserves to be felt, allowing ourselves to witness others' experience of pain at their own pace.

Feelings are relational and interpersonal embodied processes. They are meant to be felt in our bodies, and if that is hard for us, we should rely on others to help us. Understanding this is an important part of our healing journey, as many of us have been made to feel like we have to do the hard things, or the reparative things, on our own. But bringing ourselves into our feelings in an embodied way and asking for help are already a disruption to the process that created the hurt.

Stay Curious

Being able to hold our sense of goodness, even in the midst of the pain we have caused, allows us to be curious. We can reflect on our own experiences and reactions as well as the systems we exist in that perpetuated the hurt for so long. We can ask questions: What did I not know? Why did I not know it? What kept this going for so long? What would have happened if I had stopped what I was doing? What was I afraid would happen? What did I think was going to happen if I kept doing what I was doing? How might my actions have impacted other people? How can I learn what is true in ways that don't require the people I've hurt to be in relationship with me, without expecting them to owe me the story of their hurt? Are there resources that might show me how this kind of experience impacts people long term? What bigger systems are at play that keep all this covered up, or seemingly okay, for so long? What would it cost those systems to change? What would that even look like?

We can also ask, What is my relationship to power? What is my relationship to control? What is my relationship to fear? It is very hard to see ourselves clearly, especially in the areas where we have the most defenses. Doing this well can mean inviting other people to help us see what we couldn't see. We can welcome the trusted and wise voices of elders, educators, therapists, or wisdom-keeping community healers to help us look at what is hard to look at inside ourselves or in our actions. Sometimes this means searching for information from scholars, community educators, or authors who can help us learn more about the experiences of the people who were previously invisible to us. For example, if we have held ableist ideas that impacted our spiritual leadership, leading us to try to pray about people's disabilities, we might purchase the book *My Body Is Not a Prayer Request* by disability scholar Amy Kenny to help us understand where our thinking went wrong and how we can behave differently. Ideally, we do this in a way that honors the gifts and sacred wisdom of those who educate us about the places in life and culture that have caused them pain so we don't dehumanize them more in an effort to understand why we were dehumanizing in the first place.

Seek to Repair

I believe exploring the broader picture that contributed to the trauma we perpetuated ultimately encourages us to live in a good way. Educating ourselves allows us to learn from our mistakes, to tolerate the distress that comes from seeing what went wrong, and to build something better. I don't want anyone to experience suffering or the overwhelming weight of a crushed spirit, but I do believe hurt and repair are part of life and health. We can't ever be perfect, but we can learn from our mistakes and seek to grow and change. Living in such a way leaves a more gentle and loving tread on the earth and strengthens the connections we are a part of.

We are better able to repair when we have a sense of our internal worth and goodness and it endures even when we must face the hurt we have caused. Repair can look so many ways, especially in situations where the hurt is known but not encountered personally, or when we can't be in relationship with those we have hurt, or when the communities in which we caused harm continue as they always have. Repair can sometimes mean changing our actions in small and meaning-ful ways that are not just for the performance of change but allow us to head in a different direction with authenticity and sustainability. Sometimes repair means publicly acknowledg-ing our insights and plans moving forward. It can also mean stepping back and giving social space and power to those we have hurt and those like the ones we have hurt. Sometimes repair means actually seeking out the specific people we have hurt to let them know of our intention to apologize and listen to them, giving them the option to choose whether this feels useful for them or not.

Repair might mean asking a person to tell us how our actions affected them or working on ourselves and the injuries inside us that led to our defenses and hurtful behaviors. Repair might mean building new systems that operate differently than the ones we got caught up in. Repair might mean thinking about healing in a systemic way, when we have been conditioned to think of healing as individual. I often think of repair as doing the opposite of what created the wounds. Because many wounds involve a sense of being devalued or afraid or powerless, the opposite might be to witness others in a way that creates the experience of being emotionally nurtured and cared for.

There's no perfect formula, but these ideas can help us clarify where our action for repair needs to go.

◆ ◆ ◆

Recently, someone said to me, "Our relationship matters to me, and I'm glad you told me that what I did hurt you. I am so sorry. I was so caught up in what was happening for me that I didn't pause to reflect on how my actions would impact you. I am going to work hard to be thoughtful and slow down next time I'm in a situation like that. From what you've told me, I know my actions hurt you, but I want to know more about what that was like for you. If you feel like it is the right time to do so, can you tell me about how that has been lingering in you since then?"

This is not the perfect apology for all experiences, relationships, and contexts. But it mattered to me, and it repaired the wound in our relationship. They showed me they could hear about and receive my hurt, they wanted to stay connected, and they wouldn't make it all about them when I told them what hurt. They didn't get stuck in a grief or shame spiral that caused their pain about my pain to eclipse my ability to be with my hurt, which could leave me feeling the need to care for them. They didn't get defensive and explain all the reasons why they did what they did. They did the opposite of what caused the hurt; they showed me they saw what went wrong and made the space to consider my experience. And that mended something between us.

The three steps listed above are not necessarily linear. I could imagine them in a Venn diagram, overlapping and mutually influencing one another. In addition, these steps are useful no matter what you have done. Even if you are not in a spiritual context now, haven't been in the past, or are sure you have not participated in spiritual trauma for someone else, you likely need these skills, questions, and processes in some area of your life, whether a romantic relationship, a parent-child relationship, or a friendship.

· PRACTICE ·

Courage at the Core

The work of feeling pain, being open, and seeking repair all require tremendous courage. They require us to be connected to ourselves in an embodied way, feeling the security of our goodness that allows us to look at what we have done wrong: to see it differently, to hear others experiences without defaulting to defensiveness or spiraling into shame. Courage is also essential if we are seeking to break the pattern of self-silencing or cultural-silencing about our pain and spiritual trauma; it can be risky to use our voice to break an implicit group rule that told us we cannot name the wrongs and hurts. No matter how we look at it, courage is needed to shift the dynamics that keep people in the legacy of spiritual trauma.

To engage in this practice, you might begin by letting your body feel supported, shifting your posture so that you can feel yourself rooted, either through your seat or feet. Take a moment to notice how the ground, or chair, or couch, or whatever is underneath you, is holding you up. You might take a few breaths here to let yourself really push your weight into whatever is holding you up, seeing how it doesn't give way. Then, allow yourself to bring your attention to your core. Start by bringing one hand to your belly or chest and one hand to your back; see if you can feel the space between your hands. Notice the volume of your core, the density, the movement as you breathe. You might also shift your hands to your waist or ribs on either side, again feeling the space between your hands, the volume, the density, the movement as you breathe. Imagine that you can find a place somewhere inside of this contained area where your courage lives. If you want, you could also ask your body to show you where courage lives inside or around you. I like to imagine it as a long flame that runs from my pelvis up to my throat. As you make contact with your courage, you could imagine asking it what it says. You might imagine this place inside of you has a voice with words like these:

- I am able to look at how I have hurt people, I am able to feel pain of that.
- I am able to be curious and stay open to learn more, to see how I was wrong.

- I am able to make it right, to do the slow work of mending the wounds I or others have caused.
- It is an important part of growing wise and strong to feel the pain of others with them, without collapsing into a spiral of shame; this will bring healing to me, to others, and to the systems we live in.
- Even if I was wrong or hurt others, I am no less valuable or lovable. When I know this, I can be even more courageous to see how I was wrong and hurt others.

You might end the practice by thanking your body for holding this courage and knowing for a time when you would need it most.

Mark Charles on the Legacy and Healing of Spiritual Trauma

It was right around the time I started asking about how I too had contributed to the spiritual trauma of others that I found the work of Mark Charles and the book he published with Soong-Chan Rah in 2019, *Unsettling Truths: The Ongoing, Dehumanizing Legacy of the Doctrine of Discovery*. I was already aware of the history of colonization in Canada and the United States and the stolen land of the Indigenous people of Turtle Island my family and I are uninvited guests on. I had learned of the horrors of the church-sanctioned residential schools, whose ongoing effects are very real and live on today in the bodies of the survivors, their families and children and children's children, and in the cultural legacy that impacts us all. I had also learned about how the Crown had stolen land, not respected treaties made, and actively covered up genocide. I had not yet learned of the role the church had played in colonization and the genocide, abuse, manipulation, segregation, enslavement, and dehumanization of the Indigenous people of Turtle Island.

Let's just say this work was a wake-up call to me. Charles and Rah piece together the puzzle of how a nonviolent, relationally oriented, compassionate rabbi from a poor Brown family could be turned into a White, Western European icon for imperialism, exceptionalism, violence, and dehumanization. Their work helped me see how this religion that is so dear to me and part of my family legacy and cultural identity is so implicated in the spiritual harm of others. It helped me see how I am part of the web of spiritual trauma, benefiting from, even perpetuating, this system that has caused so much destruction.

At times, this has made me want to distance myself from anything that even hints of imperialist Christendom or the organized form of the religion as a whole. Other times, it has made me want to claim the identity of Christian even more, feeling the full weight of the grief along with others in my community and allowing that to be a kind of witnessing, allowing the grief to be the beginning of a metamorphosis of myself and of the systems that shaped me and caused this harm. Still other times, it has made me want to slow all the way down and see myself in the middle of this web, pain being passed down to me by my ancestors, which I continue to pass on, but also realizing that when I look at it that way, it helps me see our interconnectedness in a way that begins to heal the wounds caused by the illusion of our individuality, an illusion that's also a product of White, Western European Christendom. Here it should be noted that my reference to ancestors is both biological and spiritual. I have come to learn from others that our ancestors are not simply our blood relatives but also the people on whose shoulders or legacy we stand, or anyone we would consider our "people."

Learning this made something click about the large scope of these conversations on spiritual trauma: if the legacy of the church on Turtle Island—or North America—is built on a foundation of spiritual trauma, it makes sense that it is woven into so many expressions and the culture of our religion now. I imagine, among other things, spiritual trauma and our culpability as un-invited guests ground down into the soil of the culture of Western Christianity. If the church grows out of the soil of this history, of course spiritual trauma would be part of what springs forth. If harm, abuse, and oppression set the foundation for the history of the church here, it makes sense that more trauma would come from that; we might hardly even notice when it is happening, having been convinced it never happened or, worse, that it was God's plan.

I was moved that Mark Charles accepted my request for a recorded conversation, and I feel honored to be sharing a portion of it with you. I encourage each of you to read his work, especially his pieces addressing historical trauma and the lasting psychological impacts of perpetrating trauma.

Mark Charles

Mark [introduction in Navajo]: Yá' át' ééh. Mark Charles yin-ishyé. Tsin bikee dine'é nishłí. Dóó tó'aheedlíinii bá shíshchíín. Tsin bikee' dine'é dashicheii. Dóó tódích' íí' nii dashinálí.

Hello, my name is Mark Charles. And in our Navajo culture, when we introduce ourselves we always give our four clans. We're matrilineal as a people, and our identities come from our mother's mother. My mother's mother is American of Dutch heritage, and that's why I say Tsin bikee' dine'é; loosely translated, that means I'm from the wooden shoe people. My second clan, my father's mother, is Tó'aheedlíinii, which is the waters that flow together. My third clan, my mother's father, is also Tsin bikee' dine'é. And my fourth clan, my father's father, is Todích'íí'nii, which is the bitter water clan. It's one of the original clans of our Navajo people.

I also want to acknowledge I moved from my home on the Navajo Nation to Washington, DC, about seven and a half years ago. And where I live now is the traditional lands of the Piscataway. And I want to honor the Piscataway as the hosts of the land where I now live. I want to thank the Piscataway for their stewardship of these lands. And I want to just publicly state for your podcast how humble I am to be living on these lands today. . . .

When you look at the spiritual abuse of the church, and especially as a Native man, I look at the way that the church has literally weaponized the Scriptures and uses the Scriptures, often in ways we're not even aware of. For example, I was reading the Scripture, I was reading the Bible with my daughter several years ago. We were reading the Bible before she went to bed. We were reading the book of Genesis, and we were reading about Sodom and Gomorrah. Now I remember the lesson of Sodom and Gomorrah when I was in Sunday school with the flannelgraph. The judgment comes on Sodom and Gomorrah and Lot, and his family escapes and God says to Lot's family, "Don't turn around." And Lot's wife turns around and turns into a pillar of salt. And it's a lesson about being obedient to God and not looking back. And that was very much ingrained in me when I was in Sunday school.

But if you read that story—the whole story—God said he was going to destroy Sodom and Gomorrah. And Abraham is bargaining with God for the fate of the city because his nephew lives there. And he starts at a hundred and gets all the way down to ten, and he stops at ten because, I am assuming, he knew the size of Lot's family and that ten would be a safe number of righteous people living in the city, so if he got to ten he would save the city and save his nephew. And so the angels go into the city as men and go into Lot's house, and they're staying with Lot. As they're in the house, the men of the city come knocking on the door and say, "Send out those men; we want to be with them." And Lot, protecting the men, says to the men of the city, "Don't do this. Here, take my daughters. They're virgins." I'm reading this to my daughter. I looked at her and I said, "Honey, no man, I do not care who they are, ever has the right to speak about you or to you that way."

And the problem is we teach this lesson in Sunday school, and we pinpoint Lot's wife, who turns around and turns into a pillar of salt. And what's troubling about that is that the passage portrays a God who is more concerned about a woman who turns around than a man who pimps out his daughters. Right? If you want to understand why there's so much abuse in the church today, especially toward women, we have to look at what we're teaching in our Sunday school, where we are literally giving our young children the lesson that God is more concerned about a woman who turns around than a man who pimps out his daughters. And that's one of the seeds of incredible spiritual abuse.

And in much the same way, the Scriptures have been weaponized against people of color and other marginalized people— and especially against Natives. And we see this in the boarding schools, where the message is "Jesus is White, like the majority culture. And he really demands that you worship him in an assimilated manner. You have to learn English. You have to understand our customs. You have to give up your pagan ways. And you have to even give up your own creation stories and your relationship with Creator. And you have to embrace the creation story that's in the book of Genesis." This is where it becomes incredibly damaging.

Once the Scriptures get weaponized and you have the dominant culture using these Scriptures to oppress other people, the challenge is the people doing the oppression feel justified. The Doctrine of Discovery, the series of papal bulls written between 1452 and 1493, says things like: invade, search out, capture, vanquish, and subdue. All Saracens and pagans whatsoever, reduce their persons to perpetual slavery, convert them to His and to your use and profit. It's the church in Europe saying to the nations of Europe, wherever you go, whatever lands you find not ruled by White European Christian rulers, those people are subhuman, and their land is yours to take. The Doctrine of Discovery dehumanizes Indigenous peoples. This is the doctrine that allowed European nations to go into Africa, colonize the continent, and enslave the people because they didn't see them as human. And God calls us to love other people. So once we dehumanize them, now we can exploit them just like we feel the right to exploit the environment.

Once you take away their humanity, now you're no longer accountable for treating them well. Again, there is this Western view of creation, which is for our exploitation and profit. And so by dehumanizing African people on the continent of Africa and Indigenous peoples, this is what allows Columbus to land in what they call the New World. And even though there were millions of people living here, they claimed to have discovered it because there were no people here by their definition. We were savages. And then the narrative goes even further. And this goes back to John Winthrop when he's in the Boston colony preaching his sermon "A Model of Christian Charity." He essentially refers to what they are doing as claiming their promised lands. This "promised land" narrative, which Europeans, Pilgrims, Puritans, all these settlers use, this is what even drove the myth of manifest destiny. Once you believe that you have God's permission to claim your promised lands, you're God's chosen people and God has given you promised lands. In a plain text reading of the book of Exodus, or Deuteronomy and Joshua, you now have permission to commit genocide. God literally said to the Israelites when they went into Canaan, leave no man, no woman, no child, no animal left alive. Kill everything that breathes. So promised land for one people is literally God-ordained geno-cide for another group of people. When you have this mentality, this worldview that says you are superior—you're God's chosen people, God has given you these promised lands—that gives you spiritual justification to commit genocide.

In the United States, we called that manifest destiny. Cana-dians were a bit more polite. They didn't rebel against the Crown the way the thirteen colonies did here. But you still made it from sea to shining sea, right? . . .

The church unfortunately is horrible at looking at their own history and responding well to this. When you cause hurt, in-tentionally or unintentionally, it's a healthy response that you feel guilt. Not crippling, overwhelming guilt, but it's a helpful response that you understand you did something wrong and think, *I shouldn't have done that, and I want to make some kind of amends.* The problem is when you justify your actions or when your actions are justified for you, there's no space to deal with that guilt.

I was the driver of a car in high school where my brother was a passenger and we had a single-car accident and my brother died. I knew I was dealing with trauma. I survived the accident. I had a pretty severe head injury. I actually lost my memory of the hour before the accident, and it didn't come back until days later. All of that was my body protecting itself and trying to survive and everything else. And I knew I had been traumatized by that accident. The biggest challenge I faced, though, is every time I tried to bring up the conversation of whether the accident was my fault, well-intentioned people said, "Mark, it wasn't your fault. There was no conclusive evidence that it was anything you did wrong. This was just God's will. This was God's timing. It wasn't your fault. Don't go there." And so I was left with these incredible feelings of guilt and no place to explore them or to even feel them because every time I tried to bring them up, I was shut down by well-intentioned people who didn't want to see me go through that and didn't know what to do with what I was talking about.

Once I did this research and I found this understanding of a perpetration-induced traumatic stress, I immediately knew that's what I was dealing with after my accident. Now I found this research almost fifteen years later, but I knew that's what I was going through; I knew I was the driver of the car. I knew it was a single-car accident. It was fairly clear it wasn't a mechanical failure. And so I knew either something I did or didn't do, whether I fell asleep, whether I overcorrected for something on the road, whether I just got distracted, I don't know. This was before cell phones. I knew there was something I did or didn't do that most likely caused the accident. And to be honest, I never felt peace until I owned that. And I was able to say that something I did or didn't do not only caused the accident but resulted in the death of my brother. And I didn't get peace until I owned that and acknowledged my own actions and the consequence of my own actions or inactions.

People commit these horrific acts of violence, or these violences are committed on their behalf, and they are receiving some sort of benefit from that violence on a regular basis. And yet that violence is explained as what God expected us to do or this is what you know. There's no place to take that guilt. And I can tell you from firsthand experience that guilt is going to eat you alive until you actually deal with it and acknowledge it.

This is why I think White people get so distraught over these things, because the longer you bury psychological damage like that, the uglier it looks when it finally rears its head, and it comes out in some very destructive and painful ways. And so this is the challenge for when you deal with a lot of spiritual trauma: the church is so afraid of it because the church does not know how to deal with guilt in a healthy way. It either smooths it over quickly or just lays it on and manipulates people with it. So the people who have committed these wrongs have no place to go with their guilt, and they have no place to work through it or deal with it in a healthy way, which only leads them to continue to act and behave in unhealthy manners. . . .

The book Soong-Chan Rah wrote prior to our book is *Prophetic Lament*, which is one of the great places where we need to go once we're experiencing these types of emotions. Lament is not about repentance or even forgiveness. Lament is about sitting in the brokenness and allowing the depth of the brokenness to seep into you. Soong-Chan points out the Western church is horrible at the process of lament. It's terrified of lament. And so even if it goes there, it jumps out very, very quickly. And so we're carrying around a lot of these emotions and have had no place to process them.

The book that I wrote with Soong-Chan, *Unsettling Truths*, was reframed from our original thesis as a public rebuke of the church. And our conclusion is that the church, left and right, conservative and liberal, holds the values of the Doctrine of Discovery at a very core level. And both sides are absolutely complicit in its dehumanizing actions. And both sides believe in Christian nationalism. They frame it differently, but both sides believe in it, because, again, that's what justifies their past.

We conclude that in its current state, the church does not have a role in healing what was broken because its only solution will be to make the nation Christian again, which is not going to solve anything. And so the only option for the church to get into a place where it can actually be the healing community it was intended to be is to go through the process of lament. And not "I'm going to dip my toe in lament and take it out and say I've done something," but a lament that sits there. And one of the things that I point out is in the Scriptures and in my experience, when the people of God lament, God, Creator, always, always, always shows up. Creator does not come as quickly as most of us would like, but Creator does come. There's a whole aspect of God's character the Western church has never met because it has not stayed in lament long enough to meet God there. And if the church can stay there long enough, it can actually be transformed. But it has to be willing to sit there.

I am calling the church into a season of lament. Not a period of lament, a season of lament, because it's Creator who changes the seasons. So stay in lament longer than you feel comfortable and until Creator shows up.

One of the other damaging things to the Western church is its hyperindividualistic worldview. And I've seen this in so many of my lectures, where there's usually a White male who becomes visibly distraught, but in a healthy way. I can tell they're not going to blow up at me, but they're wrestling with things in a healthy way; they're hearing it, they're taking it in, and they're wanting to do something about it. And these are the people who, after my presentations, are usually the first ones to jump up and say, "I'm sorry" or "Can I wash your feet?" or to do something else like that. And I've learned to stop them and explain to them, first, I'm not mad at you, individually. I'm not mad at you, and your apologizing to me is not going to do anything here. The challenge is your worldview is hyperindividualistic, and you're hearing this history for the very first time. And so you literally have four-teen hundred years of oppressive history weighing down on your shoulders. And the only thing you can think of is how am I going to go to sleep tonight? So you want to apologize to me. I would have to forgive you. You could then go home to your bed in the suburbs and know that you heard about this injustice. You confronted it in yourself, you confessed it, and now you dealt with it.

Meanwhile, I'll go back to my Native community, and you'll get to enjoy the benefits of that injustice. I'll have to go home and deal with the dregs of that injustice. And nothing's changed. So, I tell them, you feel guilty? Good. You should. This history is horrific. You absolutely should feel guilty, but you have to learn how to understand, and you have to understand how to experience that guilt at a communal level, not at an individual level. And this isn't just you. This is what was done on your behalf. This is what your community has done. And you have to learn how to experience that at a communal level.

And the problem with hyperindividualistic worldviews is when you can move guilt off the individual onto the communal level. Then that's like you've been absolved of it. Right? No, you still have to deal with it. But this is something we have to correct through systemic change, not through your washing my feet or your asking me for forgiveness. This is about changing the system. And the problem is that because the church doesn't stay in lament long enough to understand the depth of the brokenness, they're then not willing to put in the work to change the system. They want a quick, simple solution because they don't understand the depth of the brokenness. And so I point the church over and over and over again back to lament. I literally have to tell the church that you can't lead this process: (a) you caused it, (b) you've weaponized your own Scriptures to justify it, and (c) this goes back to my book, you wrote Christ out of ecclesiastical history and inserted Constantine, right? You've written Christ out of your own history. So you don't have the tools you need to actually bring the healing that's necessary.

CONCLUSION

Grief Is a Form of Hope

Recently, I read the book *Liberated to the Bone* by Susan Raffo. It was medicine to me. In it she invites those in healing professions to reflect on where their lineage of care comes from. She suggests that if we feel drawn to a particular lineage of work, we ask a series of questions over and over throughout our lives, without being satisfied with easy answers. She writes:

> Who are the people who live lives that they shaped into teachings you have learned from? What happened to them? Are their descendants still freely and easily practicing these traditions, on their own terms and supported by their own elders? If they are, how can you honor these descendants and their elders, showing gratitude for how their practices have taught you? If they're not, how does this shape your gratitude? What can you do to support their descendants in any of their work to reclaim their languages, traditions, and cultural practices?
>
> Why do you feel drawn to this particular lineage? Where did you first learn about it? What did you think or hope for

when you first encountered the teachings of this lineage? What about your life experience resonated with what you're learning?

What are your people's relationship to the people who created this practice? Was there harm there? Connection and mutual learning? Distance and ignorance? If there was harm, what are you doing to repair that harm? How are you working to make sure that, as you learn and are deepened by these cultural traditions and practices, the descendants of those who gave birth to this practice are also cared for and cared about, on their own terms and in their own ways?[1]

Although Raffo is speaking about people who do healing work of various sorts, so many of these questions apply to those of us in religious or spiritual traditions. Especially if we have found ourselves within a tradition through birth or family culture or later in life through experiences of connecting deeply with how the meaning positively impacts us personally, it may be time for us to ask the questions about legacy of harm and cultural and community impact.

Reflecting on spiritual trauma has made me at times feel paralyzed. Other times I'm able to bear the weight of it without freezing and can linger in reflection. How could I, unknowingly, cause or benefit from someone's harm? How could any of us do that? I picture the pain, fear, and power of my ancestors handing down pain through a long line of people to me, and I feel the grief and fear of realizing I have already done that too, and I will continue to do that. I will hurt people without knowing it. I may even hurt people and know it, and not choose to stop it, believing what I'm doing is right. I will look away from someone who needs my help and become complicit in their wounding. I will have a safer, more comfortable existence because someone else is hurting in a system built to dehumanize them and value me, and I will sometimes pretend that isn't happening or will not even know the full extent of it. We all will.

When I sit with this longer, I realize that for me the freeze is easier than the grief of feeling it all. Grief is so painful to endure, yet such an important part of healing.

I was speaking at an event recently that was part of a visioning conference for a network of churches. When I saw the booking request and the title of their conference, I thought they must have had the wrong person; they wanted me to come talk about spiritual trauma to their network of pastors and leaders in a conference oriented toward creativity and hope? This can't be. Then something kicked in, and I realized this is the most hopeful thing! It is naming the wounds and allowing them to be felt, pulling them back out from under the rug to see the light of day. It's the systemic version of what happens in trauma therapy: at some point people seek out support because the task of navigating around all the unprocessed things actually pulls from them tremendous energy. It is life energy being used to shove things down and pretend they don't exist. It's costly to our systems, individual and collective, to ignore the hurt we've caused. As painful as the grief is, it's actually the doorway to healing and hope. It is a necessary step for mending the damage done and is less costly in the long run than continuing to pretend the pain isn't there.

Grieving the wounds we have and have been a part of and really witnessing the pain we have passed between us feels like holy work to me. It's the kind of spiritual practice I want to be a part of: one where we don't have to do it alone. We don't have to get sucked under by the weight of it.

The pathway that pain creates is like an open channel. I imagine pain, like sludge in a bucket, passed back and forth between people in a line: each person behind me an ancestor, each person in front of me a child or community member to come. Each time the bucket is handed over some sludge sloshes out, causing pain to the people and land around it. What if there were also other buckets being passed along, buckets full of water representing love, and each time it spilled out it nourished the land and was sustenance for the hard work of living? What if the route of connection between us all still existed, but resources could also be passed along this chain of joining hands? And what if we knew there would always be enough water, that more than enough of what we needed would be there?

This allows the expanded view of recognizing that resources—that love and courage and wisdom and kindness and nurturance—are also passed along this pathway, and there is everything we need in the chain of connection to face the pain, to heal from and repair it, and to keep going. This allows me to know that even though I have caused pain and will continue to, that I have the courage to face that, to keep going, and to look for where love is coming into me and through me too. I have an unwavering, unshakable belief that we are good, were created good, and are still good, even if that goodness feels very far away, or tucked deeply inside us and covered up by all the pain.

My hope is that this project was like one of the buckets of water, passed between us in a way that brings life to you, and your community, and those who come after you.

May you know deep down inside that you are good and loved, may you know spaces and connections where you are nurtured, challenged, and witnessed, and may your pain be met with love and kindness, allowing you to meet the pain of others with love and kindness. May all of this be part of our collective healing.

· PRACTICE ·
Tending to What Is Inside with Connection

It would make sense for you to need some space to tend to what is inside right now. But in service of remembering our interconnectedness, which allows us to do the tending in a transformative and sustainable way, you might bring to mind all the ways you are not alone.

First, you might start by noticing what feels useful for you right now. Would it feel better to move your body and find a way to release the energy, put your hands on your body and hold yourself, go put your feet in the grass or stare out the window for a while, or pull out a journal and pen?

Second, as you do whatever feels supportive and right in this moment, I invite you to consider a few phrases, perhaps repeating them to yourself as you move, feeling them in your hands as they are held against your chest, or writing them down. These words come from a collective practice by Ontario therapist Melissa Taylor:

I see you.
I hear me.
I feel my ancestor's stories.
My ancestors change me.
I change my ancestors.[2]

ACKNOWLEDGMENTS

The more I learn about spiritual trauma—its legacy living in me and around me—and the more I learn about how to repair these wounds in my lifetime, as well as forward in time and backward with my ancestors, the more I have deep gratitude for my interconnectedness with the people around me and the land on which I live and the more impossible it is to see myself in isolation.

To the Ləḱʷəŋən/Lekwungen (Songhees and Esquimalt) and W̱SÁNEĆ (SȾÁUTW̱/Tsawout, W̱JOŁEŁP/Tsartlip, BOḰEĆEN/ Pauquachin, WSIḴEM/Tseycum, MÁLEXEȽ/Malahat) First Nations, on whose lands and traditional territories I live and wrote this book: thank you for tending to the land and thank you for teaching me about the web of life that sustains us in both visible and invisible ways.

To Dan and Leslie, and the entire team at Sanctuary Mental Health Ministries: thank you for your encouragement and the platform with which to use my voice and the place to be supported as I named what needs to be named. This book would not have been written without you.

To my soul sisters, Alexandra, Kelsey, and Lisa: I am so grateful for each of you and your love, wisdom, and friendship. Ever consistent and growing, you are a soft and steady place for me to unlearn and change, always showing me how to trust what I know, who I am, and the goodness and beauty of living with a heart and hands wide open.

To Michael Gungor, Mike McHargue, the Liturgists listeners, and the Inglorious Pasterds: thank you for welcoming me into your communities to speak publicly about these ideas and experiences, making room for me to have a voice about what was previously unnameable or kept private for so many. You opened a doorway to even more transformation than I could have imagined.

To my friends: I cherish all our conversations about spiritual trauma—from the early stages before there were any words on paper and far into the process of refining this book. You helped me sort ideas, clarify theories, and remember what is most true about what we need as people to thrive and flourish. Thank you.

To my agent, Angela: I have come to feel so clear about what it is I'm trying to say in my own voice and why it matters. You have helped me wade through the sea of instincts, ideas, and voices sometimes not my own. I have come to see in so many ways how these projects are as much ours as they are mine.

To Julie and Katelyn at Brazos Press: I am terrified to imagine what this book would be like without your incisive editorial skills. Deep bows of gratitude to you both.

To Roberto, Mark, Alison, K.J., Joon, Mihee, Preston, and Laura: thank you for your generosity and wisdom. I have learned so much from each of you, and I continue to do so. Your words and your kind offering to this project continue to teach me about the web of interconnection that holds me. I am humbled to know you and learn alongside you.

To my mom and dad: thank you for showing me that in all the ways I am changing and growing I am still always loved and held. I will never, ever be able to fully express my gratitude to you—not just for the practical ways you support me in my work and living but for how you tend to my heart and mind. You have nurtured my desire for curiosity, play, and growth. Even when it has taken me in surprising directions, I feel you right by my side.

To Kevin, the champion, invisibly giving of our time together so I can make things that feed my soul: I'm grateful to know that with what we have built together I can have it all; I never have to choose between our love and my love for making things that go into the world.

To Audrey: I wrote most of this while you were asleep, whether day or night, and yet you were with me in every part of it and were at the very core of why I wanted to write this. To love you, to know you as you become yourself, has been the surest I have ever been that we are born infinitely good, valuable, and whole. Loving you has taught me more about what it means to be human, what it means to know God, than anything else in my life. May you always know that goodness is inside you, that your voice matters, and that your body can be trusted.

NOTES

Introduction

1. Weezer, "Undone (The Sweater Song)," track 4 on *The Kitchen Tape* (1992 demo tape).

Chapter 1 The House Is Haunted

1. Michelle Panchuk, "The Shattered Spiritual Self: A Philosophical Exploration of Religious Trauma," *Res Philosophica* 95, no. 3 (2018): 505–30.

2. *Diagnostic and Statistical Manual of Mental Disorders: DSM-5* (American Psychiatric Association, 2013).

3. U.S. Department of Health and Human Services, "SAMHSA's Concept of Trauma and Guidance for a Trauma-Informed Approach," Substance Abuse and Mental Health Services Administration, July 2014, https://nc sacw.acf.hhs.gov/userfiles/files/SAMHSA_Trauma.pdf.

4. Judith L. Herman, *Trauma and Recovery: The Aftermath of Violence—From Domestic Abuse to Political Terror* (Hachette, 2022), 48.

5. Bessel A. van der Kolk, *The Body Keeps the Score: Brain, Mind, and Body in the Healing of Trauma* (Viking, 2014), 21.

6. Peter A. Levine, *Healing Trauma: A Pioneering Program for Restoring the Wisdom of Your Body* (Sounds True, 2008), 9.

7. Gabor Maté, *The Myth of Normal: Trauma, Illness, and Healing in a Toxic Culture* (Avery, 2022), 23.

8. Saj Razvi relayed this during a training conference on Psychedelic Somatic Interaction Psychotherapy.

9. Lynne E. Vanderpot, John Swinton, and Helen Bedford, "The Unforeseen Relationship Between Spirituality and Psychiatric Medication: A Hermeneutic Phenomenological Study," *Journal of Spirituality in Mental Health* 20, no. 1 (2018): 14–26.

10. Charles MacKnee, "Sexuality and Spirituality: In Search of Common Ground," *Journal of Psychology and Christianity* 16, no. 3 (1997): 210–22.

11. Teresa B. Pasquale, *Sacred Wounds: A Path to Healing from Spiritual Trauma* (Chalice Press, 2015), 22.

12. Marlene Winell, *Leaving the Fold: A Guide for Former Fundamentalists and Others Leaving Their Religion* (New Harbinger Publications, 1993).

13. For more on adverse religious experiences, see Laura E. Anderson, *When Religion Hurts You: Healing from Religious Trauma and the Impact of High-Control Religion* (Brazos, 2023).

14. Daryl R. Van Tongeren, *Done: How to Flourish after Leaving Religion* (American Psychological Association, 2024), n.p.

15. Panchuk, "The Shattered Spiritual Self."

16. Hillary McBride, host, "The House Is Haunted," *Holy/Hurt* podcast, season 1, episode 1, Sanctuary Mental Health, July 12, 2023, https://holyhurtpodcast.com/ep-01-the-house-is-haunted/.

17. Heidi M. Ellis, Joshua N. Hook, Caleb Freund, Jacob Kranendonk, Sabrina Zuniga, Don E. Davis, and Daryl R. Van Tongeren, "Religious/Spiritual Abuse and Psychological and Spiritual Functioning," *Spirituality in Clinical Practice* (2023), https://doi.org/10.1037/scp0000346.

18. Van der Kolk, *The Body Keeps the Score*, 298.

19. Resmaa Menakem, *My Grandmother's Hands: Racialized Trauma and the Pathway to Mending Our Hearts and Bodies* (Penguin, 2017), 10.

20. Robert J. Lifton, "Understanding the Traumatized Self: Imagery, Symbolization, and Transformation," in *Human Adaptation to Extreme Stress: From the Holocaust to Vietnam*, ed. John P. Wilson, Zev Harel, and Boaz Kahana, Plenum Series on Stress and Coping (Plenum, 1988), 7–31.

21. Herman, *Trauma and Recovery*, 54–55.

22. Darryl W. Stephens, "Bearing Witness as Social Action: Religious Ethics and Trauma-Informed Response," *Trauma Care* 1, no. 1 (2021): 51.

23. Scott D. Easton, Danielle M. Leone-Sheehan, and Patrick J. O'Leary, "'I Will Never Know the Person Who I Could Have Become': Perceived Changes in Self-Identity Among Adult Survivors of Clergy-Perpetrated Sexual Abuse," *Journal of Interpersonal Violence* 34, no. 6 (2019): 1139–62.

24. Jennifer H. Wortmann, Crystal L. Park, and Donald Edmondson, "Trauma and PTSD Symptoms: Does Spiritual Struggle Mediate the Link?," *Psychological Trauma* 3, no. 4 (2011): 442–52.

25. K.J. Ramsey, *The Lord Is My Courage: Stepping Through the Shadows of Fear toward the Voice of Love* (Zondervan Reflective, 2022), 134–35.

Chapter 2 Shards of Glass

1. Biographical details about Freud are from John Fletcher, *Freud and the Scene of Trauma* (Fordham University Press, 2013), and J. N. Isbister, *Freud, an Introduction to His Life and Work* (Polity Press, 1985).

2. Jeffrey M. Masson, ed. and trans., *The Complete Letters of Sigmund Freud to Wilhelm Fliess 1887–1904* (Harvard University Press, 1985), 264 (emphasis original).

3. Fletcher, *Freud and the Scene of Trauma*.

4. Bessel A. van der Kolk, "The Body Keeps the Score: Memory and the Evolving Psychobiology of Posttraumatic Stress," *Harvard Review of Psychiatry* 1, no. 5 (1994): 253–65.

5. Robert Scaer, *The Body Bears the Burden: Trauma, Dissociation, and Disease*, 3rd. ed. (Routledge, 2014), 19.

6. Natasha Files, personal email communication, September 16, 2024.

7. Naomi I. Eisenberger, Matthew D. Lieberman, and Kipling D. Williams, "Does Rejection Hurt? An fMRI Study of Social Exclusion," *Science* 302, no. 5643 (2003): 290–92.

8. Michelle Panchuk, "Distorting Concepts, Obscured Experiences: Hermeneutical Injustice in Religious Trauma and Spiritual Violence," *Hypatia* 35, no. 4 (2020): 607–25.

9. Judith L. Herman, *Trauma and Recovery: The Aftermath of Violence—From Domestic Abuse to Political Terror* (Hachette, 2022), 1.

Chapter 3 Pulling Back the Curtain

1. Images of the Duluth Power and Control Wheel are readily available online, and I would encourage readers who are unfamiliar with it to find and review it.

2. Laura E. Anderson, *When Religion Hurts You: Healing from Religious Trauma and the Impact of High-Control Religion* (Brazos, 2023), 213.

3. Preston Hill, recorded audio interview, March 30, 2024.

4. For representative works of Urie Bronfenbrenner, see *The Ecology of Human Development: Experiments by Nature and Design* (Harvard University Press, 1979), and "Toward an Experimental Ecology of Human Development," *The American Psychologist* 32, no. 7 (1977): 513–31.

5. Joel Hollier, Shane Clifton, and Jennifer Smith-Merry, "Mechanisms of Religious Trauma amongst Queer People in Australia's Evangelical Churches," *Clinical Social Work Journal* 50, no. 3 (2022): 275–85.

6. Ilan H. Meyer, "Prejudice, Social Stress, and Mental Health in Lesbian, Gay, and Bisexual Populations: Conceptual Issues and Research Evidence," *Psychological Bulletin* 129, no. 5 (2003): 674–97.

7. Bessel A. van der Kolk, Alexander C. McFarlane, and Lars Weisaeth, eds., *Traumatic Stress: The Effects of Overwhelming Experience on Mind, Body, and Society* (Guilford, 2007), 279.

Chapter 4 All in the Family

1. Adam Young, "Revisiting the Big Six: What You Needed from Your Parents," *The Place We Find Ourselves* podcast, episode 159, accessed July 14, 2024, https://adamyoungcounseling.com/revisiting-the-big-six-what -you-needed-from-your-parents/.

2. Allison Cook, "The Role of Reflective Judgment in the Relationship between Religious Orientation and Prejudice," PhD diss. (University of Denver, 2011), https://digitalcommons.du.edu/cgi/viewcontent .cgi?article=1789&context=etd.

Chapter 5 How We Feel

1. You can learn more about drama triangles through an online search, or if you want to dig deeper, see Eric Berne, *Games People Play: The Psychology of Human Relationships*, 2nd ed. (Nicholas Brealey, 2017), and *Transactional Analysis Psychotherapy: A Systematic Individual and Social Psychology* (Ballentine, 1975).

2. If you are interested learning more about in Bowen's work but would prefer not to read a textbook on family therapy, I recommend Michael Kerr, *Bowen Theory's Secrets: Revealing the Hidden Life of Families* (Norton, 2022).

3. For more on AEDP, I recommend reading Hilary Jacobs Hendel, *It's Not Always Depression: Working the Change Triangle to Listen to the Body, Discover Core Emotions, and Connect the Your Authentic Self* (Spiegel & Grau, 2018). If you don't mind something more on the academic side, I would suggest the most recent textbook edited by Diana Fosha: *Undoing Aloneness and the Transformation of Suffering Into Flourishing* (American Psychological Association, 2021).

4. See John Welwood, "Between Heaven and Earth: Principles of Inner Work," in *Toward a Psychology of Awakening: Buddhism, Psychotherapy, and the Path of Personal and Spiritual Transformation* (Shambhala, 2000), 11–21.

5. Audre Lorde, "The Master's Tools Will Never Dismantle the Master's House," in *Sister Outsider: Essays and Speeches* (Crossing Press, 1984), 110–13.

Chapter 6 Seeing and Believing

1. Judith L. Herman, *Trauma and Recovery: The Aftermath of Violence— From Domestic Abuse to Political Terror* (Hachette, 2022).

2. Karen O'Donnell and Katie Cross, eds., *Bearing Witness: Intersectional Perspectives on Trauma Theology* (SCM, 2022).

3. Shelly Rambo, *Spirit and Trauma: A Theology of Remaining* (Westminster John Knox, 2010), 5.

4. Rambo, *Spirit and Trauma*, 9.

5. Herman, *Trauma and Recovery*, 135.

6. Darryl W. Stephens, "Bearing Witness as Social Action: Religious Ethics and Trauma-Informed Response," *Trauma Care* 1, no. 1 (2021): 49–63.

7. For more about this way of conceptualizing our inner worlds, see Carol Gilligan, *In a Different Voice: Psychological Theory and Women's Development* (Harvard University Press, 2016), and Richard Schwartz, *No Bad Parts: Healing Trauma and Restoring Wholeness with the Internal Family Systems Model* (Sounds True, 2021).

8. Emily McIntosh, host, "Lostness, Trauma, and Stories of Transformation with Bayo Akomolafe," *Transforming Trauma* podcast, episode 71, June 1, 2022, https://narmtraining.com/transformingtrauma/episode-071/.

9. Rambo, *Spirit and Trauma*, 9.

Chapter 7 Mending and Meaning

1. Daryl R. Van Tongeren, C. Nathan DeWall, Sam A. Hardy, and Philip Schwadel, "Religious Identity and Morality: Evidence for Religious Residue and Decay in Moral Foundations," *Personality & Social Psychology Bulletin* 47, no. 11 (2021): 1550–64.

2. Preston Hill, recorded audio interview, March 30, 2024.

3. My friend Kurt once called Jesus a "first century Jewish Mystic," and I loved it so much it stuck. This is my rendering of Jesus's words written in Matthew 16:25.

4. Craig S. Cashwell and Paula J. Swindle, "When Religion Hurts: Supervising Cases of Religious Abuse," *The Clinical Supervisor* 37, no. 1 (2018): 182–203.

5. Rosemary de Castella and Janette Graetz Simmonds, "There's a Deeper Level of Meaning as to What Suffering's All About: Experiences of Religious and Spiritual Growth Following Trauma," *Mental Health, Religion & Culture* 16, no. 5 (2012): 536–56.

6. Kelsey D. S. Siemens, "Embodiment of Spirituality and Sexuality: Women's Lived Experience of Resilience to Sexual Shame" (PhD diss., Trinity Western University, 2015).

7. Alyson M. Stone, "Thou Shalt Not: Treating Religious Trauma and Spiritual Harm with Combined Therapy," *Group* 37, no. 4 (2013): 323–37.

8. Stone references the works of several theorists, including D. W. Winnicott, *The Maturational Processes and the Facilitating Environment: Studies in the Theory of Emotional Development* (1965; repr., Routledge, 2018), and Ana Maria Rizzuto, *The Birth of the Living God: A Psychoanalytic Study* (University of Chicago Press, 1979).

9. Hill, recorded audio interview.

10. David Augsberger, *Caring Enough to Hear and Be Heard: How to Hear and Be Heard in Equal Communication* (Regal, 1982), 12.

11. Ranier Marie Rilke, *Letters to a Young Poet* (Norton, 1962), 35.

Conclusion

1. Susan Raffo, *Liberated to the Bone: Histories, Bodies, Futures*, Emergent Strategy Series (AK Press, 2022), 138.

2. I learned this from Melissa Taylor directly during a clinical training session.

HILLARY L. McBRIDE (PhD, University of British Columbia) is a registered psychologist, an award-winning researcher, former cohost of the *Liturgists* podcast and current host of the *Other People's Problems* and *Holy/Hurt* podcasts. She has a private practice in Victoria, British Columbia, and is a sought-after speaker and retreat leader. McBride is the author of *The Wisdom of Your Body, Practices for Embodied Living*, and *Mothers, Daughters, and Body Image*. Her work has been recognized by the American Psychological Association and the Canadian Psychological Association.

CONNECT WITH HILLARY

hillarylmcbride.com

⬤ @realhillarymcbride

⬤ @hillaryliannamcbride

⬤ @hillarylmcbride

⬤ @hillaryliannamcbride